D0064981

presented to:

Leslie

from:

Jan & Cam

date:

May 2012

What people are saying about

Simple Little Words

"If you want an enjoyable and rewarding experience, read this book and ask God to make you the kind of person who says a word of encouragement to those you meet. They will be better for it, and so will you. I loved reading this book!"

—TIM LaHAYE, NEW YORK TIMES BEST-SELLING
AUTHOR AND MINISTER

"Simple words. Sometimes they flow so easily, the speakers don't realize the impact of their words. Yet those words can change attitudes, shift direction in life, offer hope, or thoroughly crush the hearers. In this book, nearly forty people share the words that changed their lives or the impact their statements made on others. I finished this book with the thought: What we often think of as simple words become powerful when spoken. We never know the impact of what we say."

—CECIL MURPHEY, WRITER/COWRITER OF MORE THAN ONE
HUNDRED BOOKS, INCLUDING THE NEW YORK TIMES
BEST SELLER *90 MINUTES IN HEAVEN* AND
GIFTED HANDS: THE BEN CARSON STORY

"Get out the tissues and get ready to be inspired. Simple Little Words will not only change your life, but it will equip you to change others' lives for the good in small ways that make a BIG difference!"

—PAM FARREL, AUTHOR OF OVER TWENTY-FIVE BOOKS INCLUDING
BEST-SELLING *MEN ARE LIKE WAFFLES, WOMEN ARE LIKE
SPAGHETTI* AND *WOMAN OF INFLUENCE*

"Wow! Michelle Cox and John Perrodin offer captivating stories about the power of encouragement in Simple Little Words and show us how to make that same difference in another's life. But don't start this book before you are supposed to leave for a meeting. You won't want to stop reading."

—SANDRA P. ALDRICH, AUTHOR OF
FROM ONE SINGLE MOTHER TO ANOTHER

simple little words

simple little words

what you say can change a life

michelle cox & john perrodin

SIMPLE LITTLE WORDS
Published by Honor Books®, an imprint of
David C. Cook
4050 Lee Vance View
Colorado Springs, CO 80918 U.S.A.

David C. Cook Distribution Canada
55 Woodslee Avenue, Paris, Ontario, Canada N3L 3E5

David C. Cook U.K., Kingsway Communications
Eastbourne, East Sussex BN23 6NT, England

David C. Cook and the graphic circle C logo
are registered trademarks of Cook Communications Ministries.

The Web site addresses recommended throughout this book are offered as a resource to
you. These Web sites are not intended in any way to be or imply an endorsement on the
part of David C. Cook, or the authors, nor do we vouch for their content.

The names of some characters have been changed for privacy reasons.

All Scripture quotations, unless otherwise noted are taken from the New King James
Version. Copyright © 1982 by Thomas Nelson, Inc. Used by permission. All rights
reserved. Scripture quotations marked msg are taken from THE MESSAGE. Copyright
© by Eugene H. Peterson 1993, 1994, 1995, 1996, 2000, 2001, 2002. Used by
permission of NavPress Publishing Group.

ISBN 978-1-4347-9997-5

© 2008 Michelle Cox and John Perrodin

The Team: Susan Tjaden, Theresa With, Jack Campbell, and Susan Vannaman
Cover/Interior Design: The DesignWorks Group
Cover Photo: © Y. Nakajima/Getty Images

Printed in Canada

First Edition 2008

1 2 3 4 5 6 7 8 9 10

With love to my husband, Paul—my sweetheart, my best friend, and my biggest cheerleader.

To my sons, Jeremy, Tim, and Jason—the joy of my life.

To my daughters-in-law Lydia and Laurel, and my soon-to-be daughter-in-law, Kella—the answer to a mother's prayers.

And in loving memory of Rev. Ralph Sexton Sr., whose prayers and encouraging words touched my heart and life. I miss you, Popie.

—*Michelle Cox*

For Sue. You are a precious creation, marvelous mother, wonderful wife, and beautiful friend. Please know that my simple little "I love you" encompasses so much more. Thank you, sweetie!

Also to my powerful, potent arrows: Tad, Cosette, Quentin, Carol, Patch, Jenna, and Jace. God blessed me when he made me your dad. You are priceless gifts from him.

To my parents, Tom and Helen. Please know how much I love you. Thanks for giving me encouragement through the years.

To my sister, Julie, her husband, Tim, and their children, Taylor and C.J. May God ever bless and protect you.

To my brother, Mark, his wife, Dina, and little Bethany. May you keep seeking his will.

—*John Perrodin*

And a word spoken in due season,
how good it is!

Proverbs 15:23

CONTENTS

ACKNOWLEDGMENTS

A book like this doesn't happen without the help and cooperation of many people. We're grateful for this opportunity to thank the special individuals who have been part of making *Simple Little Words* become a reality.

Thank you to our amazing editor, Susan Tjaden. She has made working on this book such a pleasure. Every author should be so blessed! Thank you to all the staff at David C. Cook. You are an awesome group and we enjoy working with you. A special thanks to Don Pape, Ingrid Beck, Kate Amaya, Amy Quicksall, Denise Washington, and the fantastic sales and marketing team who work so hard to place our book in the hands of readers.

We deeply appreciate best-selling author Jerry B. Jenkins taking the time to write a foreword for our book. What an honor!

Thank you to the special people who were kind enough to share their stories. We know God will use your experiences to touch hearts and lives.

We send a huge thank-you to the world's best prayer team: Terenia Autrey, the Bell family, Greg Bentley, Tatyana Buksh, the Cox family, Jeannie Day, the Gordon family, Doug Guy, the Hess family, Crystal Holden, Mary Jane Hollyday, Steven James,

Debbie and Lynn Kaupp, the Kracht family, Aileen Lawrimore, the McCoy family, Danielle McEntyre, the Morgan family, Kerma Murray, the Neville family, Connie Norris, the Osten family, the Perrodin family, Davis Plemmons, Debbie Presnell, Bev and Vern Reinertson, Amy Rickman, Jeremiah (Bub) Shelton, Lorraine Sherlin, Margaret Skiles, Mary Jo and Bob Steinke, Wade Stephens, Aaron and Missy Sumner, the Trinity Baptist Singles, the Vetsch family, Dianne Waggoner, Lavonia Whitson, and Jeanie Young. You are the strength behind our writing. You've been such an encouragement, and we could not do this without you. God bless you abundantly for your faithfulness.

A special thank-you to the Blue Ridge Mountains Christian Writers Group, and to our readers, Margaret Skiles, Aileen Lawrimore, and Laurel Cox, for their suggestions and corrections as we worked on this project.

We would be remiss if we didn't thank our spouses and children for their help and support as we spent long days glued in front of our computer monitors. Thanks for your patience. We love you.

Last but not least, thank you to the God who gave us the dream and then equipped us with what we needed to accomplish the task.

FOREWORD

When we were kids and complained of being teased, we were told, "Sticks and stones may break my bones, but words can never hurt me."

Now we're adults and we know the truth: "Sticks and stones may break my bones, but words can break my heart."

Why is it that if we get a dozen evaluations of our work—eleven good, one bad—the one we obsess over is the bad one?

As a lumbering twelve-year-old, trying to get used to my changing body, I nearly fell going downstairs. An adult said, "Nice play, ox."

But I'll get over it. It was only forty-five years ago.

Why are true compliments so precious? Because they are so rare. Be the one who encourages, who says something someone is not likely to hear from anyone else.

So often, the highest praise is the simplest. Professional athletes don't gush over each other's spectacular feats. They merely shake their heads and say, "He can play."

An opponent throws a runner out at the plate from 350 feet away, and one will shake his head and say, "That's an arm."

As a fifteen-year-old fledgling sportswriter, I waited

anxiously as an editor read my article. No drums, no music, no ovation, no embrace, no smile. Just, "You can write," and it appeared in the paper the next day. And I haven't quit writing since.

Be the one who speaks those simple little words.

—*Jerry B. Jenkins*

INTRODUCTION

Words are powerful. They can inspire, encourage, and remind the weary that they are loved. Or they can wound, tear down, and daunt the spirit. What we say can change someone's life forever. That is the crux of *Simple Little Words.*

When we began writing this book, we received lots of encouragement. People liked the idea of reading uplifting stories. But when we asked friends to share their own anecdotes, the results were fascinating.

Some people immediately thought of a story, its impact forever embedded in their hearts and minds. Others had to think for a few days before a story surfaced. Many people couldn't recall even a single instance when another's words lightened their hearts. Sadly, nothing sweet had lodged in their memories.

I (Michelle) was a child from a dysfunctional home situation that left me with no self-confidence and no self-esteem. And then a friend's parent made a comment. Her simple little words changed my life. For the first time, I saw something beautiful in myself. The moment occurred almost forty years ago, but I remember it today as vividly as if it happened yesterday.

I've worked with teenagers and young adults for over thirty years. During those years, I've made a conscious effort to say something positive to each young person with whom I've come in contact. I've had the privilege of watching them blossom as their lives were touched by simple little words.

The same sort of impact is possible in the workplace. I (John) have always strived to see the possibilities in those around me—even in those whom others may have labeled "difficult." With gentle words I've allowed people to discover gifts they didn't realize they had.

Both of us realize how crucial it is to nurture the people closest to us with words of encouragement and affirmation—our spouses, children, grandchildren, and friends.

Dive into *Simple Little Words* and emerge refreshed. Discover how crucial every word can be … both for you and those within the sound of your voice.

Visit us at www.simplelittlewords.com. We'd love to hear from you.

Oh, and just in case these stories about simple little words touch your heart—and bring tears to your eyes—remember to grab a tissue so the pages don't get wet.

SELF-ESTEEM

THE MOST BEAUTIFUL GREEN EYES

MICHELLE COX

A word fitly spoken is like apples of gold in settings of silver.
—PROVERBS 25:11

Every time I looked into the mirror, the image that looked back at me was ugly. At my advanced age of eleven, I was convinced of that. I wasn't just unsightly on the outside, I saw myself as unattractive on the inside, too.

Numerous life events, including a dysfunctional home situation, had contributed to my low self-esteem. Well, maybe not *low* self-esteem. *Nonexistent* would be a more apt description.

My home life fell apart when my parents divorced soon after my sister's death. Overwhelming grief flavored their days, and laughter and fun disappeared from our home. Friction and angry scream fests ensued.

Several months later, all our belongings were packed and my

dad moved to one city, and my mother and I moved to another city far away.

My mom developed severe emotional problems, and I spent many nights cowering in fear as she lashed out at me and broke things while screaming, "You're worthless. You'll never amount to anything." And in my childish heart, I believed the hurtful things she said. Words that smashed my self-esteem.

That's why I looked in the mirror and saw only shame and ugliness—repulsive on the outside, and worthless on the inside, too.

Then something happened that changed my outlook on life forever.

Our teacher had scheduled a field trip for the class. The sun shone bright on that perfect spring day. Several moms had agreed to drive, and I was part of the group assigned to Mrs. Fincannon's car. I ended up sitting in the middle of the front seat next to her.

Getting everyone settled in the car took a few minutes. While we waited for the others to take their places, Mrs. Fincannon looked at me and smiled. Then she said, "You have the most beautiful green eyes I've ever seen."

I'm sure the moment was just another trivial instant long forgotten by Mrs. Fincannon, but those ten simple little words she said to me that day changed my life. I'm sure she never realized her words would have that kind of impact, but I was a child who needed to hear those words, and almost forty years later, they are still as clear in my heart and my memory as if they were spoken yesterday.

You see, for the first time, this child whose heart had been battered and bruised, saw something of beauty in herself. Maybe—just maybe—I wasn't so ugly after all. Maybe I wasn't worthless.

That was a turning point in my life. Mrs. Fincannon's words left such an impression that I've spent the last thirty years working with young people, bolstering hearts that have been battered and bruised by life and home situations.

I always make it a point to say something positive to them, to give them a sincere compliment. I've had the pleasure of watching them blossom as many of them—for the first time—see something of beauty in themselves.

I always smile as I remember the lesson learned from Mrs. Fincannon so many years ago—that our simple little words can touch hearts and change lives.

Words—so innocent and powerless as they are, as standing in a dictionary, how potent for good and evil they become in the hands of one who knows how to combine them.

—NATHANIEL HAWTHORNE

Dear Lord,

Please help me never to speak words that will wound the lives of others. Help me to be an encouragement to those I encounter, a shining reflection of your love and mercy. Remind me that my words can make a difference in the lives of those I meet along life's way.

Amen.

HOPE

ONE WORD MADE ALL THE DIFFERENCE

DENNIS E. HENSLEY, PHD
—professor and author

Let your speech always be with grace, seasoned with salt,
that you may know how you ought to answer each [other].
—COLOSSIANS 4:6

In my capacity as a professor of English at Taylor University Fort Wayne, I teach a survey course in world literature that students of all majors are assigned to take as part of their liberal-arts requirements.

A few years ago, I met Sean, a junior and wrestling-squad member who was majoring in elementary education. Sean had a shaved bullet head, legs like fire hydrants, a back that could put Atlas to shame, and biceps that looked like the drawing on boxes of Arm & Hammer Baking Soda. This guy was tough.

Sean enjoyed sports, and he excelled at weightlifting and track-and-field events, such as discus and hammer throwing.

However, he wasn't overly keen on literature. I knew quickly I'd have my work cut out in making him an admirer of Keats, Shakespeare, Dante, and Melville.

I modified Sean's reading list for that semester to include high-seas adventures by Jack London, mysteries by Sir Arthur Conan Doyle, and military works by Rudyard Kipling. We met in my office once each week to discuss the books and short stories, and I constantly praised Sean's ability to recognize symbolism, foreshadowing, flashbacks, and other elements of literary expressions that I had lectured about in class.

As the semester advanced, so did Sean's grades. He had started as a C student, then rose to the B level. As I showed the class how the applications of literary analysis could help them better appreciate plays and movies, they all became more and more eager to get to class each day. Sean started sitting in the front row, taking copious notes, and I continued to compliment him on his diligence and studiousness.

Then, one day, as I was grading papers, I was delighted to be able to give a perfect A to Sean on one of his quizzes over a new short story I'd had the students read for that week. At the end of the quiz I wrote, "This is superb work, son. I congratulate you. You've been working hard, and this is the payoff. Well done!"

I passed the papers back, and I watched as Sean's face lit up in a grin when he saw the huge red A atop his quiz. However, when he turned the page over and read my personal note to him, his countenance changed entirely. He lowered his face, avoided eye contact with me the entire rest of the class, and left just as soon as the bell rang. I was thoroughly confused by such behavior until two days later.

During office hours, I glanced up to see Sean's hulking frame taking up my entire doorway. "Can I come in for a moment, Dr. Hensley?" he asked me. I motioned him toward a chair, and he closed the door behind him. I could see that he had his quiz in his hand.

"Sir," he began, but then stopped. He lowered his head, and suddenly I realized that this giant of a man was actually weeping. I was stunned. I gave him a moment to collect himself. "Sir, you don't know my background."

I said nothing as Sean fished a handkerchief from his back pocket and wiped his eyes.

"My dad left my mom and me when I was only seven," Sean said in a low voice. "I somehow felt it was my fault that he left. I got it into my head that if I could just be a better son, my dad would come back and live with us again. We'd all be happy then."

He paused, then added, "So, I played every sport at my schools and all the summer sports I could sign up for. I thought that if I could just hit enough home runs or score enough touchdowns or shoot enough baskets, my dad would be proud of me and would come back."

"Did it work?" I asked gently.

Sean shook his head. "My dad only showed up at three of

my games during ten years that I was involved in sports. It was no big deal to him. I tried my best to impress him, but I always felt that I'd failed. I haven't heard from my dad for the past two years, and I probably never will. I thought I had gotten past caring, until …"

I leaned forward a little. "Until what, Sean?"

"Until I got my quiz back from you day before yesterday," he said, looking directly at me. "You praised me … and you called me *son*. You might have meant it just as a passing catchphrase from an older man to a younger fellow, but it hit me like a freight train. I realized at that moment, that all my life I've wanted to have a man whom I looked up to, to tell me he was proud of me and to call me *son*. You have no idea what this note on this paper means to me. I plan to keep this for the rest of my life."

Sean wiped another sudden rush of tears from his eyes.

"I came here to tell you something, Dr. Hensley. I want you to know that I am going to conduct my life from here on out— in everything I do—so that you will always be proud enough to call me *son*. I won't ever let you down. I promise you that. You've given me something that I've been yearning for my entire life, and I want to protect it."

He rose, and so did I. I shook his hand and gave him a manly hug, concluding with a slap on the shoulder. "You're a fine man, Sean," I assured him. "I have no doubt you'll make me proud of you in whatever you do in life."

A year later, Sean graduated with his degree in elementary education. He passed the licensing examination for Indiana and took a job in one of the worst elementary schools in inner-city Indianapolis. Most of the students there were from single-parent families, and all were desperately poor. Sean became a surrogate father to many of them. He would take his old van into the projects and ghettos and pick up dozens of children and take them to sporting events, Saturday movies, or vacation Bible school. He called the boys "son" and the girls "daughter," and they loved it.

In calling Sean "son," I not only changed his life, I gave him a focus on the ministry he wanted for his lifetime calling. He's now changing the lives of hundreds of other fatherless children.

Yes, indeed, one word of encouragement can change the world.

The hope is always here, always alive, but only your fierce caring can fan it into a fire to warm the world.

— SUSAN COOPER

Dear Lord,

Put someone in my path today that needs to hear that someone cares. Please give me the words to encourage them and to make a difference in their life. Thank you for those who have invested in me by providing words of comfort, hope, and inspiration when I've needed to hear them.

Amen.

GUIDANCE

DIVINE DIRECTION

KAREN KINGSBURY—*award-winning inspirational author*

I can do all things through Christ who strengthens me.
—PHILIPPIANS 4:13

I had made a decision to give up writing.

All my life I'd been writing, whether stories or newspaper articles or poetry. I wrote for my junior high creative magazine and my high school newspaper and yearbook. I wrote in my journal, and I scribbled poems in my spare time.

I went into my first year of college intent on more journalism, more writing. But I had a fallout with my high school boyfriend, and I spent more time sitting on Zuma Beach trying to get over the breakup than I did in class. At the end of the year, the university sent me a notice—I was on academic probation.

That summer was a time of soul-searching, and finally—for reasons I can't even remember now—I figured I would return to the local junior college and get serious about school. I would study to be an attorney or a legal assistant, something new and exciting, something different. In my first semester that fall, rather than take English, I opted for journalism—an easy A, I thought.

The first few assignments were brief and didn't take much work. But then we needed to write a feature story on a family whose home was destroyed by a fire. I loved writing features, and I was happy with my story when I turned it in the next day.

Later that week the professor—Bob Scheibel—handed back all the hundred stories from our class, and everyone received his or her paper. Everyone except me. As the class ended, he called me to the front of the room. I couldn't understand what I'd done wrong or how I'd landed on his radar so early in the course of the semester.

With concern I walked up to his lectern, eyes wide.

"Two things," he said. He was an older man, a veteran journalist with a gruff tone and a sharp tongue.

I gulped. "Yes?"

"First … you will never, ever stop writing." The words filled the room, surrounding me with a truth that was indisputable both because of the manner with which he spoke, and the knowing that resonated in my soul.

He waited, measuring the fact that his words had hit their mark. Then he took a slow breath. "Second … you will see me tomorrow morning at eight a.m. at my office. You'll be joining the school's newspaper staff immediately."

God, in his infinite wisdom, in his amazing ability to know the plans he has for each of us, had placed Bob Scheibel in my life at just the right time. I did as he asked; I joined the staff of the *Pierce College Round-Up*, and later that semester I competed in a journalism contest and won first place in state for feature writing.

I thank God for Professor Scheibel, and his few strong words. Simple words that filled me with a sense of direction and knowing. Words that—in a moment's time—changed the course of my life.

Wise words can ripple through
a soul and change a life.
— MICHELLE COX

Dear Lord,

Make me sensitive to your leading and give me a willing heart that will obey you with joy. Open my eyes so I will see your plan for my life. As you open doors for me, help me to be ready to walk through them. More than anything, when I come to the end of my life, I want to hear you say, "Well done."

Amen.

DREAMS

INSPIRED BY WALT DISNEY

MCNAIR WILSON—*former Disney Imagineer*—AS TOLD TO MICHELLE COX

"For I know the thoughts that I think toward you,"
says the LORD, "thoughts of peace and not of evil,
to give you a future and a hope."
—JEREMIAH 29:11

Most grown men don't carry a pouch of colored markers in their briefcase. For McNair Wilson, that's as natural and normal as breathing. McNair is—well—he's different. Where most of us see the world in sedate greens, and browns, and blues, McNair's world explodes with vivid reds, purples, and yellows.

Ask McNair what he was like as a child, and he'll answer, "Just like what you see now." And after spending time with him, one soon understands that while the outward facade is that of a man, his heart and soul still feel the childlike delight of each new adventure.

Young McNair was a dreamer. Sometimes his larger-than-life self overflowed into other people's worlds, and adults—not understanding his creative genius—endeavored to make him conform like other children.

His uniqueness was apparent early on. He was the child who rearranged his goldfish bowl each week when he cleaned it. Sometimes the castle would be on the left, sometimes on the right—and sometimes, upside-down.

His bedroom was also different. As he tells it, "I put the bed at one end of the room, and placed a screen in front of it where the bed couldn't be seen. The rest of the room was my office and waiting room. I had a guest book for everyone who visited," he remarks nonchalantly, as if every little boy had a guest book in his bedroom office.

McNair's dad was a member of a navy reserve unit that met one weekend a month. The year Walt Disney was the Grand Marshal of the Tournament of Roses Parade, the navy arranged an event so the reserve members' children could meet Mr. Disney and get his autograph.

McNair's mom did the decorating. She made her famous punch and tinted it to match the gown of the Rose Parade Queen. Everything came together in fine form for the momentous day.

When Walt Disney arrived, he went through the catering line and then proceeded to the autograph session. When someone mentioned that Mr. Disney needed a chair, McNair quickly volunteered to find one. As he pushed the chair across the polished floor, it slipped from his grasp and thudded into Walt Disney's shin, eliciting a sharp grunt of pain.

Hanging his head in embarrassment, McNair slunk to the far side of the room, wishing the floor would open up and swallow him.

The room soon emptied. McNair raised his head, a shamed expression coloring his features. "I'm sorry I hit you with the chair."

"That's okay. Come over here."

McNair retrieved his sketchbook and shuffled across the room.

Mr. Disney asked, "What's your name?"

"McNair Wilson, sir."

"What do you have there?'

"It's my sketchbook, Mr. Disney."

"Could I see what you've drawn?"

He leafed through the colorful artwork. "These are great, McNair. Would you like me to autograph your sketchbook?"

Soon the signature of the great Walt Disney graced the simple pages of the book.

"Well, McNair, what do you like to do?"

"I like trains, Mr. Disney."

"I like them too."

And for the next few moments, the world famous man and a curly-haired little boy just sat and talked about model railroading.

"I like trains, Mr. Disney, but I *really* like to build buildings."

"Do you use a kit or do you build your own?"

"Oh, I like to build my own. You know, like that guy, Claude, on *The Wonderful World of Disney*."

"You mean Claude Coats? He creates and builds backgrounds and sets. He's one of my Imagineers. Have you heard of them before, McNair? They design and build hotels, and shopping centers, and everything in our theme parks. They even design the landscaping." Mr. Disney smiled at the fascinated little boy.

"What do you want to be when *you* grow up, McNair?"

With wide-eyed wonder, McNair said, "I want to be an Imagineer."

Walt Disney leaned over, emphatically poked McNair on the shoulder with one finger, and said, "And so you shall."

And with those simple little words, a dream was planted in the fertile soil of a young boy's heart and imagination.

Many parents would have squashed that dream, encouraging their child to consider something more normal, more realistic. But not McNair's parents. They cultivated the dream, watering it daily with words of encouragement.

One day his mom asked, "McNair, why don't you write to that Claude guy?" And the tender shoots of hope continued to unfurl as a young boy fed his dream of becoming an Imagineer.

Fast-forward twenty-something years and those carefully nourished aspirations exploded into a colorful garden of reality as McNair began his job as a Disney Imagineer. For the next ten years, he lived his fantasy, designing and building fanciful theme parks.

Now, McNair spends his days as a corporate creativity coach, conference speaker, actor, and author, inspiring others to dream their dreams—and God's dreams—for their lives, to reach for what seems impossible, and to believe Walt Disney's simple little words, "And so you shall."

If you don't do *you*,
You won't get done,
And the world—Creation—will be incomplete.
But when you do you …
You *inspire* me!
—MCNAIR WILSON

Dear Lord,
Open my eyes to your plan for my life. Let me live big
dreams for you, trusting you to equip me with what I
need to accomplish those tasks. Give me a willing heart
and a joyful excitement as I seek to fulfill the plan for
which you created me. And give me words to encourage
others as they seek your dreams for their lives.
Amen.

TOP 10 THINGS YOU WISH YOUR PARENTS HAD SAID TO YOU

I love you.

You can do it.

I'm so proud of you.

I'm glad God gave you to me.

You are priceless.

I was wrong.

I'm sorry.

I'm thrilled you married such a wonderful spouse.

I love being with you. You're fun to talk to.

You are a blessing to everyone who knows you.

STEPPARENTING

I Promise to Love You

John Perrodin

I will not leave you nor forsake you.

—Joshua 1:5

For years, Sarah had struggled to raise a rambunctious and beautiful dark-eyed daughter … all by herself. Unmarried, she received no support—financial or otherwise—from the father. After the way he treated her when he heard the news of the pregnancy, she didn't want him around.

Sarah had missed having a husband's love and support, but she'd done her best to provide a happy home for her tiny daughter. And Grace had been the joy of her life, her sweet laughter and bright smiles painting each day with sunshine.

There had been some painful moments the last few years, now that Grace was old enough to notice that other children had daddies to play with them—and she didn't. Sarah remembered one particular instance on the playground when Grace had watched her friend's daddy pushing his little girl on a swing, both of them laughing as she squealed, "Higher, Daddy, push me higher."

Grace hadn't said anything, but Sarah had seen the wistful expression on her face. And she'd felt the stab of pain in her own heart because she couldn't fix the situation.

Yet she always had dreams for the two of them, dreams that someday a man would love her with all his heart, and for her little girl, the hope that someday a man would love Grace as a father should love a child.

That day had finally arrived, and within the hour, Sarah and Roger would exchange the vows that would bind their lives together. "Grace, today's our special day—for all three of us!" Sarah smiled as her daughter snuggled close on her lap.

A drop of moisture fell onto Sarah's hand. Her heart clenched as she realized Grace was crying. "Honey, what's wrong?"

"Will he … love me?" Grace choked out, fear evident in her voice.

"Of course, sweetie. Why wouldn't he?"

"My real daddy … didn't want me." The next words tumbled out in a rush. "He never called or visited or sent me a birthday card. I don't even … know where he lives."

"Oh, Grace. I'm so sorry. But things are going to be different now. Roger loves you. You'll see." She hugged her close then wiped the tears from her daughter's soft cheeks. "Today's going to be a happy day—the first of many happy days. C'mon, let's put our pretty dresses on. You're going to look beautiful."

Sarah wore a white beaded gown, lacy as any wedding-cake bride, and eight-year-old Grace was a miniature of her mother, except her dress had big pink roses to match the bouquet she'd be carrying.

Hundreds of happy butterflies took wing in Sarah's stomach as the first strains of the "Wedding March" filled the sanctuary. She watched an eager wave of friends rise to catch a glimpse of them, the bride and her bridesmaid, clutching bouquets of white and pink roses. Sarah hadn't wanted to weep but couldn't help it.

The aisle from the back of the church to the altar was the longest journey of her life. Memories of nights in prayer, empty cupboards, working late, and reading torn library-book favorites to Grace tumbled in her mind. The steep climb had been treacherous at times, but then Roger entered her life. She never doubted that the man God had given her was an answer to prayer.

Sarah glowed with joy as she saw Roger standing at the front of the church, waiting for her—for them. He looked so handsome in his black tuxedo, and once again, she thanked God that she was marrying the man of her dreams.

When she and Grace reached the altar, Roger stepped forward and Sarah waited for him to clasp her hand and stand beside her. Instead, he walked around her and knelt beside Grace, looking her straight in the eyes. The church was silent, the guests aware that something special was happening.

Standing beside her daughter, Sarah could feel Grace's shoulders quivering. She could sense her daughter's fears that Roger might have changed his mind—that he might not want *her* for a daughter.

Roger took Grace's hands in his. Then he spoke in a clear voice loud enough for everyone to hear, "Grace, I promise to love you—to love your mother always and to always be there for you. I'll never leave you—ever. And I *will* stay with you both. Forever."

Sarah watched her daughter's face, seeing the dawning wonder as Roger's sincere words seeped into her soul, filling the empty places in her heart, and making the long suppressed dream of a little girl come true—that she'd have a daddy who would love her forever.

You came into my life as my stepfather.
Then you stepped into my heart as my dad.
—MICHELLE COX

Dear Lord,
Please help me to be there for my family, to be faithful,
loving, and kind. Bind my family into a strong, secure
unit. Fill our home with your love. Thank you for
blessing us with each other.
Amen.

Remember Who You Are

Tatyana Buksh

I was struggling with a decision one day, and I went to talk things through with one of my coworkers. Arlene had often been a source of encouragement to me—even on occasions when I hadn't realized I needed it.

On this particular day, I told her about a situation I was facing, and she looked at me and said, "Remember who you are—daughter of the Most High. Never settle for anything less than what your Father would have you do."

Arlene has since moved away to take care of her elderly mother, and I've lost touch with her. But what she said is etched in my heart, and whenever I'm faced with difficult decisions, I hear her words, "Remember who you are …"

CARE

God Cares for You

Jim Daly—*president and CEO of Focus on the Family*—as told to John Perrodin

*Then they cried out to the LORD in their trouble,
and He saved them out of their distresses.*

—Psalm 107:19

Jim Daly, the president and CEO of Focus on the Family, can't brag about having grown up in the perfect family. Instead, he was like the little boy standing outside a house, nose pressed against the window, gazing wistfully at the warm family scene inside. Perhaps that's why so many who've heard his amazing story connect with his gritty realness.

Jim lived through things that most of us will never experience. His childhood memories aren't warm fuzzy ones of bedtime prayers, cookies and milk after school, or playing ball with his dad. His memories are best forgotten, the type from which tragic movies are made. This wounded little boy could only imagine what it must feel like to be part of a warm, loving family.

Young Jim witnessed unimaginable, terrifying events—such as the time when his crazed father chased his mother, Jan, around the house with a hammer in a drunken rage, intending to kill her. This was the final straw in the tumultuous marriage, leading to the divorce that split his family when he was only five.

The next few years were even tougher. Despite his mother working two or even three jobs to put food on the table and keep a roof over the heads of her five children, there were days when there was nothing to eat. Yet things became even worse for Jim when his mom remarried a few years later and the family moved to the rough streets of Compton in East Los Angeles.

A murder—most likely gang-related—took place mere feet outside eight-year-old Jim's bedroom window. The turmoil inside the walls of the house wasn't much better. Jim's stepfather, Hank, resented sharing his new wife with her children. Hank was obsessed with Jan, wanting to keep her all to himself. In fact, when she was stricken with cancer that year, Hank locked the children out of her room and tried to prevent them from seeing her.

It wasn't long before the dreaded cancer took Jan away from young Jim forever. And on the day of her funeral, Hank walked out, leaving the five children home alone.

Jim's older brothers knew a family that offered foster care. Unfortunately—though it's hard to imagine—the situation there was even worse, adding fresh scars to a little boy's battered and bruised heart. This child who needed to feel loving arms wrapped around him, and to hear words of comfort, instead felt rejection and abandonment as he moved to twenty-three different homes.

His brothers and sisters didn't have the answers. They couldn't provide the comfort he needed. But there were a few bright rays of hope during those dark days. Jim rejoices that his mother accepted the Lord hours before she died, all because of their next-door neighbors—a couple Jim knew as Grandma and Grandpa Hope.

When his mom died, the Hopes told him, "God is with you." Simple little words that made Jim feel part of a loving family and gave him an inkling that he might not be completely forgotten.

For a lonely young boy, those words meant the world to him. Even though nothing seemed to be working out right, he caught a blurry glimpse of God's larger picture. He exists. He cares. And he was concerned about Jim's ultimate destination in life.

Jim hungered to have someone care—someone who put him first instead of seeing him as an annoyance. Until he heard those words, "God is with you," he thought for sure he was completely and totally alone.

Friends like Grandma and Grandpa Hope weren't the only ones who passed along words of encouragement. Teachers and coaches also put an arm around him. "God cares for you." That message made him smile inside.

In fact, those comforting words formed a refrain that he heard often. God placed perhaps a dozen different people in Jim's life with this message of hope between the time his mother died and the time he accepted Christ at age fifteen.

For a boy who felt he had no one, the idea of a heavenly Father who cared gave Jim hope. Those simple words, "God cares for you," made him realize that God had a plan and purpose for his life.

How ironic that this man whose childhood was filled with broken promises, rejection, insecurity, and violence is now dispensing hope, healing, and help to hurting families. When Jim Daly tells families, "God cares for you" and "God is with you," they aren't empty words. They're said with conviction from a man who discovered firsthand that God was *always* there for him.

God never made a promise that was too good to be true.

—Dwight L. Moody

Dear Lord,
Thank you for your promise that you'll always be with
me. I've felt your loving arms around me on so many
occasions as I've walked through difficult circumstances.
Help me to reach out to others who need to experience
your love and compassion.
Amen.

STRENGTH

The Rest of My Life

Mary E. DeMuth—*Christy nominated author*

> *One thing I do, forgetting those things which are behind and reaching forward to those things which are ahead, I press toward the goal for the prize of the upward call of God in Christ Jesus.*
>
> —Philippians 3:13–14

When my husband, Patrick, and I first started dating, I didn't tell him about my upbringing. Prior to that, as an insecure overproclaimer, I'd spent many years recounting every little detail. I'd share my story with anyone—not because I enjoyed describing what happened in my childhood, but because I hoped to garner attention.

"Wow," people would say, "you sure endured a lot."

I lived for words like that.

But something shifted in me. As God healed me, I no longer

needed to tell my story to gain sympathy; instead, I relished *God's* attention and encouraging words.

That was enough.

Eventually I shared everything with Patrick.

The abandonment I felt when I was left alone as an only child.

How afraid I was in an unsafe neighborhood.

The sexual abuse I experienced at the hands of neighborhood boys when I was five.

The premature death of my father when I was ten.

My mother's three divorces.

All of it spilled out in a messy, painful heap. Still, Patrick loved me. Still, he married me.

Years into our marriage, though, those cracks in my heart started leaking. Tears that had been bottled up for more than a decade cascaded through the fissures.

I had problems connecting deeply with Patrick and our children. As my daughters turned five years old, I relived the nightmarish sexual abuse I'd experienced at the same age as a kindergartner. I withdrew, and even affection became difficult for me.

During this time, Patrick gave me a painful, but helpful, word picture. "You're standing on a high dive, and the kids and I are swimming and laughing in the pool below. We ask you to jump in and join us. You pace back and forth, back and forth on the high dive, but you don't jump. Instead, you back down the ladder and settle for sticking your toe in the water while we laugh and splash."

At that juncture of my life, his pivotal words opened my eyes to my need for healing. I'd naively thought that the earlier healing of not having to tell my story had been enough, like I could check "God's healing of Mary's past" off my list of life lessons and gladly move on. But Patrick's word picture haunted me. It made me want to get well.

Jesus asked a paralyzed man that same question in the fifth chapter of John. This man had been ill for thirty-eight years, and now he waited for an angel to stir the waters at the Bethesda pool. If only he could dip even a finger into the angel-churned waters, he'd be healed. I'd been like that man. I'd hoped for an instant, easy healing, where very little effort on my part was required. While the man was waiting, Jesus stood before him and asked, "Do you wish to get well?"

Patrick's illustration was Jesus' question to me. "Mary, do you wish to get well?" Because I understood my own personal pain was affecting the lives of my children and husband, I spent two years in counseling trying to understand my splintered heart and asking God to please, please, please fix my broken places.

In the midst of this heart wrestling, Patrick startled me with a few more sentences.

"Mary, I want the second half of your life to be better than the first. I'm committed to helping that come about."

Once again, I'd been languishing in the past. With Patrick's future-laden words, I started believing that by God's grace, the last half of my life *would* be better than my childhood—that the future might just be irresistible.

Healing came slowly. It continues today. Patrick's words of encouragement changed the course of my life. I'm no longer looking behind me, fretting over the past and the things I couldn't change. I'm learning to move forward on the high dive, to believe God will give me the strength to dive into the lives of my family.

This half of my life *is* better, and because of Patrick's words, I can hold his hand as we walk into the irresistible future.

Let the past sleep, but let it sleep on the bosom of Christ, and go out into the irresistible future with Him.

—OSWALD CHAMBERS

Dear Lord,
Give me the desire to get well. Heal me and help me to let the past sleep. Enable me to let go of the pain and to rest in your capable hands. Help my future to be better than my past—more spiritual depth, more excruciatingly beautiful times with you, more healthy relationships. I love you. I need you. I rest in you.
Amen.

NEED

I NEED YOU

EDNA ELLISON—*speaker and author*
—AS TOLD TO MICHELLE COX

And my God shall supply all your need according to
His riches in glory by Christ Jesus.
—PHILIPPIANS 4:19

Edna Ellison had one goal in mind: Her daughter's wedding was going to be perfect. Like most mothers-of-the-bride, she had planned for months, organizing every detail with drill-sergeant precision.

She wished her husband was still alive to enjoy this special moment in their daughter's life, and she missed his broad shoulders as she carried the weight of the responsibility alone.

The wedding day neared and Edna met with the floral designer to discuss the final details for decorating the church. "Edna, why don't we use fresh greenery and magnolia blossoms for the front of the sanctuary?" the florist suggested. "You can probably find a magnolia tree in your neighborhood, and it will save you some money. We'll decorate the day before the wedding, and then we can turn the air-conditioning really low so the blossoms will stay fresh until after the ceremony."

Edna agreed. After they decorated the sanctuary, the church looked as beautiful as Edna had imagined it in her dreams.

The next morning, Edna and her future son-in-law arrived at the church. The temperature that day was a blazing 107 degrees. Upon opening the church doors, a blast of hot air hit them instead of the refreshing coolness they had expected. They discovered that a storm during the night had knocked the power out and the air-conditioning had been off.

Edna entered the sanctuary and was horrified to see that the once glossy white magnolia blossoms were now wilted and black.

She panicked. Turning to her future son-in-law, she said, "What will we do? We can't have people come to a wedding with black flowers—and we only have a few hours until the ceremony!"

"Drive around and find whatever flowers you can and bring them back."

Edna drove through the neighborhood surrounding the church and finally saw a magnolia tree in the distance. She pulled in the driveway, rushed from the car, and knocked frantically on the door.

When an elderly man answered, she blurted, "I need you." She quickly shared the wedding-disaster story.

The eighty-six-year-old man grabbed a step stool; then he cut the blossoms and handed them to Edna. She thanked him profusely.

As she turned to leave, he said, "You don't realize what just happened here."

She looked at him quizzically. Tears welled in his eyes as he explained, "My wife died on Monday. Tuesday night, we received friends at the funeral home down the road." A trail of tears trickled down his wrinkled cheeks. "We buried her on Wednesday, and on Friday, all my children went home."

He struggled to get the next words out. Edna grasped his hand, waiting for him to finish.

"Now it's just me, and the house is so empty. I fed my wife every bite the last few years, and she doesn't need me anymore. My children are gone and they don't need me, either. I feel so alone. Right before you came, I shook my fist at God and shouted, 'God does *anybody* need me?' As the words left my mouth, you knocked on the door and the exact words you said were, 'I need you.'"

In a halting voice, he continued, "While I was cutting the magnolia blossoms for you, it dawned on me that maybe I can have a flower ministry. I noticed at the funeral home that some of the caskets didn't have flowers. I could take some for them. And maybe I can take some flowers to people at the nursing homes and hospitals to help brighten their days."

Edna wiped the tears from her cheeks, overwhelmed as she realized that God had fine-tuned the details of *her* child's wedding day so that one of *his* hurting children could hear the words "I need you."

Maybe we could minister to those in need—
if we'd just let God interrupt our day.

—MICHELLE COX

Dear Lord,
Open my eyes to those who are in need of a helping hand,
a listening ear, and a loving touch. Help me to be a
conduit of your loving hands. Thank you for supplying all
my needs and for always being there whenever I need you.
Amen.

HONESTY

Truth Sweetened with Love

Stacie Ruth Stoelting
—singer, speaker, and author

The wise in heart will be called prudent,
and sweetness of the lips increases learning.
—Proverbs 16:21

As a thirteen-year-old vacationing in Branson, Missouri, I received a coupon too alluring to ignore. A session at a recording studio. Something I'd always wanted to do.

My family took an hour out of the day to let me fulfill a dream.

At the office, I painstakingly perused the dog-eared menu, trying to decide on the perfect songs to record.

"I'd like to sing 'Amazing Grace' and 'How Great Thou Art.'" I gulped.

"Go into that booth," replied the bored employee.

"Do you think that they're good selections for me?" I wanted affirmation. Insecurity gnawed at me.

"They'll be great," the man said scratching at a T-shirt seam.

With heart outpacing the music, I clutched the lyrics. The booth seemed smaller than a restroom stall.

My sweaty palms left prints on the lyrics. My allergies made singing more difficult. It was too late to back out so I prayed, then sang with all my heart.

What a breakthrough! I was so happy. My first recording session. I'm sure my braces glistened under the lights as I smiled. My adolescent awkwardness vanished momentarily as we waited for the copies of my songs.

I hugged the recording like a jewel. "I'm done," I announced to my patient parents and sister.

"We can't wait to hear it!"

In the car, it seemed to take forever for the music to load and then finally, it began to play. I eagerly gauged reactions. The faces around me showed that something was very wrong.

My precious mom spoke first. "You want me to be honest with you, right?"

I wasn't sure. "Yes," I replied.

"I want you to always know that I'm honest and supportive. That way, you will take it seriously whenever I compliment you." She plunged on. "Right now you aren't able to sing well, honey. God has given you ability, but you need to practice. You will go far!"

While those words might seem harsh to some, to me they

planted seeds in the soil of my soul. Mom inspired me to work harder. To learn to pray while I sang.

Fast-forward seven years—almost to the day. Another performance, another chance to practice prayer-singing.

Again, my heart raced with the music. I paused to dedicate the moment to my family, friends, and mostly to my Lord Jesus Christ. Once more I sang my heart out.

But this wasn't a cramped booth. My solo was for the president of the United States, Mr. George W. Bush, and more than 11,000 other listeners.

In my teens, my mother meant what she said, "Right now you aren't able to sing well." And she was honest. God used her to spur me on. Make me try harder.

Thanks to her willingness to speak the truth with love, I have had opportunities to tape with Grammy-award winners. I recorded a demo in Ricky Skaggs' studio. God has allowed me to sing on radio, TV, and even in front of the U.S. Capitol Building.

With each CD I complete, I know my family will be as supportive of their beloved twentysomething as that nervous thirteen-year-old.

Sometimes words hurt before they help. I'm glad my mom always tells me the truth mixed with great big doses of love.

Honest words are swallowed more easily when coated with love.

—Michelle Cox

Dear Lord,

Help me to speak the truth with those I love and help me to say those words with kindness. Thank you for your tenderness as you pinpoint areas of my life that need repair. Give me a wise heart that will accept your instruction, and help the final result to be a life that will please you.

Amen.

I'm Not Who I Was

Brandon Heath
—Dove-nominated songwriter

Remembering is hard for me.

Sometimes I wonder if my mind is working properly or if I'm just your typical artistic space cadet. There are things that I wish that I could remember—where I left my phone last, what was that cool restaurant in downtown Minneapolis, and what was that lyric idea I had in the rental car last week?

Then there are things I don't want to remember. Middle school. Mom and Dad's divorce. My first heartbreak. So I tuck those memories away. But every once in a while they resurface. It was one of those memories captured in an old photograph that inspired the song "I'm Not Who I Was." I don't know where they are now, but the photo reminded me that I needed to forgive them whether they wanted it or not.

I'm not ashamed to tell you about who I was, or more importantly who I am now, in Christ. Writing a song provides one of the best ways for me to examine my soul. Writing it out in words helps me to really understand it. So, in this case, I allowed this photograph to reacquaint me with shame and regret. It immediately uncovered the memories that I thought I had forgotten.

So I had a choice in that moment. I could continue to suppress and withhold some bitterness and forgiveness and pretend not to feel the pain, or I could let it in and feel. Really feel. As soon as I did let it in, God took hold and said, "This is who you were. Now, you are a son of mine."

The experience was an opportunity in the love of Christ that transforms and cleanses us. In response, the only thing I had left to do was give the grace that was freely given to me by writing the song. It felt great. It took about twenty minutes to write. When my roommate walked in, I sang it for him. He smiled and said, "That's good."

Forgiveness is good. Change is good. Remembering is good. *God* is good. I'm so glad I found him.

Now, if I could just find my phone....

DIRECTION

An Unexpected Direction

Sandra Glahn—*author and adjunct professor*

But one thing is needed, and Mary has chosen that good part, which will not be taken away from her.
—Luke 10:42

Many generations after Eve, Ella begat Velma, who begat Ann, who begat Sandra.

I am Sandra. And the genes of my ancestors, passed on since the beginning of humanity, stop here. I will never give birth.

As the fourth of five children, and the one who most loved to babysit, I never once imagined in my youth that I might someday face infertility. I grew up in a noisy household—pretty much the community meeting place—where someone was always bickering over what TV show to watch on our one black-and-white television, or arguing over who got to talk on our sole telephone, or begging a ride off of a friend because we had only one car.

Our house was never a place for quiet reflection. Someone was always practicing an instrument (we had two string bass, one violin, one viola, one Autoharp, and one ukulele player) or having friends over to play "Life" or "Twister" or "Monopoly."

I learned early to eat leftovers cold because if I heated up last night's pizza, someone would invariably catch a whiff and proceed to the kitchen to demand that I share. To get it all for myself, I had to be discreet.

Despite the insanity of it, I loved growing up in a family of seven. I never recall anyone complaining of loneliness. When I performed in a concert, I always had a cheering section. When I received my high school diploma, I recognized the voice of my brother Steve making cuckoo noises from the top of the stadium. I relished the seven-part harmonies on our long road trips across America.

Though I went to college, I had no intention of pursuing a career. I dated my high school sweetheart, and I knew even in my freshman year that I would marry this guy. My main goal was to be a mommy. It was all I ever really wanted.

When I was twenty, Gary Glahn and I tied the knot. Having only one brother, he came from "the quiet family." Picture the matchup of large and small, loud and quiet in *My Big Fat Greek Wedding*, and you get a pretty accurate idea of the adjustments ahead.

After five years of marriage, during which Gary earned a master's degree in theology, we decided it was high time to expand our little family of two. But a year went by with no success. And then another. Finally, I went to the doctor. A third year passed.

And then it happened—the positive pregnancy test.

We were thrilled. Yet elation turned to agony soon after that when I miscarried. Then it happened again. I had a positive test, but we lost that one, too. And then another. And another. And another. We had seven early pregnancy losses. After that, we pursued adoption, but in three year's time, three adoptions fell through.

That led to a crisis. Spiritually, I wondered if God was punishing me for some reason. Emotionally, I felt unstable, with hormones fluctuating wildly. But the greatest trauma of all was my crisis of womanhood. What was I supposed to do and be?

I had always heard that a woman's highest calling is motherhood. Where did that leave me? When I went to college, I didn't go to prepare myself for a career. To be honest, I didn't really believe in women having careers.

As I write that now, it still astonishes me, as I consider how narrow my perspective was. I left no room for the apostle Paul's statement that the unmarried state, if chosen for eternal purposes, is a higher calling than marriage.

Where would my view have left tent-making Priscilla? Or the woman in Proverbs 31 who, though a wife and mom, sold belts and real estate? Or Lydia, the seller of purple from Thyatira? I didn't see then what I do now—that godly womanhood cuts its fabric from a varied pattern book, and its garments are not "one size fits all."

I had a college degree in Biblical Studies. I had equipped myself to be the best wife and mother possible, to raise my kids to know the living God. But we had no kids. And no prospect of having any. Ever.

And I could cook meals and clean floors for only so many hours a day before wondering, *If our Lord said we need laborers in the harvest and I'm sitting here with more Bible training than most pastors in the world, why am I inside all day? Shouldn't I be helping to answer the cries of the world outside my domicile?*

At that point, both my spiritual mentor and my husband encouraged me to attend seminary. They recognized in me a gift for teaching that I myself didn't see. Couldn't they see that I didn't want to teach the Bible to grown-ups? I just wanted to be a mommy!

To my amazement, the Lord provided the money for tuition. So reluctantly, I enrolled in classes. But I still had serious doubts.

I awoke the first day of class fighting nervousness as I got ready. When it came time to leave, I still had nagging doubts.

As I walked through the living room on my way to the car, I stopped. I simply couldn't go without peace. I had to know I was making the right choice. So I slipped to my knees in front of the couch. And I prayed (more like begged). "Lord," I said, "if this is not what you want me to do, please stop me. I just want to do what you want."

Has God ever spoken simple words to you? He certainly

answered me that day. I didn't hear an audible voice, but the words memorized years earlier that came to my mind may as well have been. He said, "Mary has chosen what is better."

I thought of the story behind the words from the tenth chapter of Luke. Martha is in the kitchen doing the traditional "girl" thing. She's being domestic. Meanwhile, Mary sits at Jesus' feet learning theology. When kitchen-girl complains that student-girl has messed up priorities, Jesus sets her straight. Mary has chosen what is better.

Shocking.

I got up knowing exactly what I was supposed to do. I knew seminary was where God wanted me. Those six simple words changed my life.

Today, fifteen years later, Gary and I are the proud adoptive parents of one daughter. And I teach at Dallas Theological Seminary. If you had told me twenty years ago that I'd have an "only child" and teach at a graduate school helping to train pastors and ministry workers, I would have laughed. Out loud. And shaken my head at you. Maybe even my finger.

Motherhood is a high and noble calling. But it is not the only calling. Or even the definitive calling. I've found that following Jesus Christ wherever he leads is the ultimate calling.

"Mary has chosen what is better."

God has a dream for each of us. Wouldn't it be a shame to miss it?

—MICHELLE COX

> *Dear Lord,*
> *Your words are the best words of all. They give life and direction and peace. Help me to follow you no matter where you lead. And help me to hold my plans in open palms, always ready to change them at your prompting. Fill me with your life-giving words that I might obey them and pass them on so they can make a difference in the lives of those I encounter.*
> *Amen.*

THE NOTE OF ENCOURAGEMENT

Use a note of encouragement to talk about a particular trait that you find admirable in another. Simply find a blank card and jot down a few lines thanking that individual for what they've done to help you or others. Let them know that they're doing a great job, that they've improved a situation for you, or that you are praying them through a difficult time. Nothing complicated. Just an opportunity to put your heart on paper and tell someone that you appreciate who they are … and the wonderful way they serve others. Let them know you noticed. It'll mean the world to them.

JEALOUSY

Overcoming a Negative Word

Ann Kroeker—*author*

Not returning evil for evil or reviling for reviling, but on
the contrary blessing, knowing that you were called to this,
that you may inherit a blessing.

—1 Peter 3:9

During field day in sixth grade, I sprinted full blast down the lanes to win the 50-yard dash. I loved pouring every bit of myself into that race—panting, sweating, and feeling the blood coursing through my veins. It was exhilarating.

So the next year, I eagerly joined the junior high track team and trained as a sprinter. I showed promise in the 100-meter and 200-meter dashes, the 400-meter and 800-meter relays, and the long jump. By the time I was in eighth grade, I was one of the top sprinters on the team and looked forward to running with high school athletes.

I joined the high school track team my freshman year and

started training for the spring season. I dreaded the stair laps and jogging around the track in the blustery spring winds, but I was happy to be part of things and looked forward to making new friends. I hoped to fit in. And I couldn't wait to race again.

When spring arrived, we won our first few meets, and I was delighted to contribute to our success with something that came naturally to me and brought me such joy. What's more, I thought I had found a group of high school girls with a common interest.

After one of the away meets, we were all on the bus chattering with excitement about winning. The coach stood and motioned for our attention. He gave a little speech about how proud he was and how well every girl had done.

Then he started passing out the ribbons. He was a soft-spoken guy, so it was surprising and fun when he acted like a sports announcer, calling out the place, the event, and then pausing before shouting each name. Everyone stomped, cheered, and rocked the bus for each girl as she walked up the center aisle to claim her ribbons.

He saved me for last. I'd placed first in each event that I'd entered.

"And now," he began, "with a first in the 100-meter dash … the 200-meter dash … the 400-meter relay … *and* the long jump … *Annie Hopper!*"

I walked to the front of the bus to claim my ribbons, a tad embarrassed at the attention. Then I realized that the bus didn't sound right. No one was stomping. Nobody cheered. I didn't hear any shouts of praise.

Instead, I heard a sound. When I took the ribbons and turned around, I realized that the sound was a word. One word.

"Boooooooo."

My team was booing me.

Clutching my ribbons, I plopped onto an empty seat at the front of the bus, sank down low, stuck my knees against the bench in front of me, and tried to disappear. After the bus lurched into motion, my coach slipped over and apologized.

He had hoped it would be a moment of encouragement and success for me. He suspected they were jealous, especially with my being the newcomer, the freshman.

I couldn't even look at him. He asked me questions, but I couldn't open my mouth to speak. I stared at the back of the gray vinyl seat.

One short, powerful word crushed my spirit.

That one word made it clear I wasn't accepted as part of the team. Their rejection set me apart from the rest of the bus-rocking, cheering, supportive crowd. Even though my efforts helped the entire team succeed, they told me how they felt—this particular winner was a loser.

Although they never booed me again, I never fully trusted the others, and I struggled with self-esteem. I could hardly celebrate when I felt that the team disapproved.

At least one good thing came of it, however. I resolved that I would never treat another teammate like that when I was an upperclassman, even if someone joined the team and beat me every time. I would encourage her, no matter what.

When I was a junior, a freshman sprinter did join the team, and she beat me several times. I don't know if my words meant anything to her, but I tried to remember to throw an arm around her after the race and say, "Great job. Great race. Congratulations."

I doubt if I was familiar with 1 Peter 3:9 at that time, but I somehow knew in my heart that I didn't want to answer that early insult with another insult. I wanted instead to pass on a blessing.

One humiliating, painful word rumbled through that bus when I was fifteen. At some point in the years that followed, I hope I passed on a blessing instead.

Jealousy is a disease that erodes the soul but words of blessing are a sweet balm that soothes the spirit.

—MICHELLE COX

Dear Lord,

Give me a sweet and loving nature that will rejoice with others during good times and will weep with them during difficult times. Keep me from jealousy or envy. Help me to remember how abundantly you've blessed me and help me to be a blessing to those with whom I come in contact.

Amen.

Backhanded Encouragement

Pat Neville

My grandma had been watching me do wind sprints in hopes of gaining speed and endurance. "Hey, Patrick, did you know your uncle was a great runner when he was in school?"

That was news to me. I couldn't wait to see my uncle. Maybe he could help *me* become a great runner.

When my uncle came walking out to where I was practicing, I was ready for his wisdom and eager to do anything he thought would help me improve.

His words surprised me. "Patrick, speed is something you are either born with or without, and you were born without."

Most people would think those were words of discouragement, but my uncle knew his ten-year-old nephew quite well, and he recognized a certain personality trait in me. He knew I would take the words as a challenge to prove him wrong.

That started me on a running career that lasted ten years—over five thousand miles—and helped pay my way through college. Sometimes there are different ways of using encouraging words to someone who's got a lil' rebel in him.

HOSPITALITY

You're Part of Us Now

Susie Shellenberger—*author and editor of* BRIO *magazine*

For I was hungry and you gave Me food; I was thirsty and you gave Me drink; I was a stranger and you took Me in.

—Matthew 25:35

I was out of college and away from home
for the first time.
Conway, Arkansas.
Didn't know a soul.
Till she invited me over for dinner.

When I arrived, she led me to the table and said,
"Susie, this will always be *your* place.
We want you to be part of our family.
This place will be set for you every single night.
If you get a better offer,

Or want to be alone,
That's fine.
But your place will still be set—
whether you come or not."

Then with growing conviction, she added,
"Understand what I'm saying:
When you come over, we're not going to scramble around and
set your place.
It will always be set.
You're part of *us* now."

I'll never be able to articulate how much security that gave me!

And when she hung a Christmas stocking
with *my* name on it above her mantle
and stuck *my* photo on her fridge
with stuff her kids made in school …
I felt I was genuinely connected.
To a family who cared.

She gave me belonging.

Though I will always smile when I think of
Gunsmoke snacks, Crayons, and Big Chief tablets …
the images I draw strength from were our prayer times together.

Hearts united in conversation with our Creator God.
Times we'd stay up past midnight talking
theology
and
Scripture
and
doctrine.

Through the years and across the miles,
I've probably told a million people
that she's the most creative person I know.
But there's something that goes far beyond
her creativity.
And that's her steadfastness.
Which brings me back to our friendship.
For thirty years she has prayed with me,
Laughed with me,
Cried with me.
Because of that steadfastness,
I know she's a friend committed to the long haul.

All because of those simple little words spoken over
a table with an extra place setting.

Thank you, Susan Woodard.

A plate heaped high with love and friendship will satisfy
the appetite of every guest.

—MICHELLE COX

> *Dear Lord,*
> *Help me not to worry because my house isn't spotless or*
> *I'm not a gourmet cook. Remind me that there are*
> *hungry souls who won't notice the dust or the peanut*
> *butter sandwich because their more urgent hunger is just*
> *to know that someone cares. Help my home to become an*
> *oasis for those who need a warm and loving welcome.*
> *Amen.*

SELF-IMAGE

A Precious Gem

Sandi Banks—*author*

The words of a man's mouth are deep waters;
The wellspring of wisdom is a flowing brook.
—Proverbs 18:4

On this particular day, God had turned a café into a classroom, and the eighty-year-old woman sitting across from me in the sunlit booth was to become my teacher, my friend.

I had flown to North Carolina to speak to her church group and instruct them on the curriculum offered by our ministry. Little did I know *I* would be the student instead as we met for lunch and began getting acquainted. I learned first off that her name was Beatrice. Beatrice Pearl. But everyone called her Bea.

Raised in New England, Bea had moved to the South and was a delightful lunch companion on this beautiful autumn afternoon. She began recounting some remarkable experiences from her eight decades of life. I studied her animated countenance as she reminisced about past events—the joys … the sorrows … the fun times … the hard times.

Then a pained expression crossed her face. Her mind and emotions had punched *rewind*, harkening back to a small turn-of-the-century schoolhouse classroom. Words. Harsh words. Words spoken to her as a six-year-old by a cruel teacher.

Tears welled in Bea's eyes as she recalled the day her teacher slammed a paper down on her tiny desk, pointed to a word on it, and demanded, "What does *that* say?" "Oh, that says 'Pearl,' ma'am. That's my middle name," little Beatrice beamed.

"Well," snapped the teacher, "don't you write that name until you can *shine* like one."

Bea's lips quivered, her voice faltered as she tried to choke back the surge of welling tears. I wept with her, and we sat silent for a long while—my heart aching at the painful, lifelong scars inflicted by that mean-spirited teacher.

Eventually I learned that it had been another thirty-one years before she could even write her middle name without crying. Her older brother finally helped her through the process.

My hand reached for hers as my mind reached for answers: What if that teacher had used the same energy, the same number of words, to relay a different message?

"Pearl? That's a precious gem. One day you will shine like one."

One dozen words and a heart broke. One dozen words and a heart could have bloomed.

Plant words of kindness and watch a garden bloom.

— MICHELLE COX

Dear Lord,
Help me to remember that the words I speak
each day are powerful tools. Guard my lips from hurtful
or angry words. Instead, help them
to provide comfort, cheer, compassion, and
hope for those who need to hear them.
Let my words please you in all that I do.
Amen.

MARRIAGE

In Sickness and in Health

Michelle Cox

This is My commandment, that you love one
another as I have loved you.
—John 15:12

Theodore Todd was physically small in stature, but in every way that really mattered, he was one of the biggest men I've ever known.

I first met him when I was a little girl. We attended the same church, and whenever the doors were open, Mr. Todd was there, usually attired in a polyester-checked sport coat and a felt fedora hat that he tipped in a courtly manner whenever he greeted one of the ladies.

Under most circumstances, Mr. Todd was one of those people who faded into the background, his quiet nature and unassuming manner never the type to draw public attention.

He and his wife, Clara, had married back in the '30s, standing before God and each other as they repeated the words of their marriage vows, promising to love each other "in sickness and in health, till death do us part." For the next sixty-four years, the two were completely devoted to one another, their close relationship made even more so because they didn't have children.

They took pride in their garden each summer, canning and freezing enough of the bounty to share and to carry them through another winter.

They often invited other churchgoers home for Sunday dinner where they received a warm welcome and plates piled high with Clara's fine home cooking.

And so life continued for many years. Then things changed abruptly when Clara suffered a stroke. Mr. Todd tended her with loving care, watching her decline as a second stroke further decimated her weakened body. A third stroke arrived, this one more debilitating than the previous, and it soon became apparent she would need more medical care than he could give.

He grieved when Clara moved to the nursing home a few miles from their bungalow. She was the love of his life, woven into his heart; and now half his heart was no longer home.

The house was so empty. For almost sixty years, Clara had filled their home with love and laughter. Now silence echoed throughout the rooms. He missed the simple things. Reaching over to kiss her in the morning. Talking together about the birds that played outside their window. Telling her "I love you" as he went to bed.

There was never any question that he would honor his wedding vows, those words "in sickness and in health" so lovingly spoken many years before.

His days took on a new routine that lasted for seven years. Each morning, he would drive down the street, walk the gleaming halls of the nursing home, and spend the day with his Clara, tenderly wiping her face, rubbing lotion onto her dry hands and feet, and talking about the precious times they'd shared before illness invaded their lives.

Where most people walking past Clara's door would have just noticed a frail, elderly woman in a hospital bed, Theodore Todd still looked at her with eyes of love that saw the beautiful bride he had married so many years before.

The only day Mr. Todd varied from his routine was on Sunday when he honored his other lifelong commitment, sitting on a pew at Trinity Baptist Church, filling out a tithing envelope in his shaky handwriting, and worshipping the God who had been his and Clara's strength throughout their lives.

At 11:45 sharp, he would slip quietly from the pew, and those of us sitting near him would wipe tears from our cheeks. We knew where he was going. We knew it was time for lunch with his precious Clara.

And we knew we'd been privileged to witness a lesson in love as Mr. Todd honored those words, "in sickness and in health, as long as we both shall live."

True love is where two hearts and lives are so entwined that you can't tell where one begins and the other ends.

—MICHELLE COX

> *Dear Lord,*
> *Please help me to honor my marriage vows. Thank you for entrusting my spouse to me. Remind me that each day we share together is a special gift from you. Help our lives to be a lesson in love to those around us.*
> *Amen.*

GRACE

BLESSED LIMITATIONS

SHERRIE ELDRIDGE—*speaker and author*

And He said to me, "My grace is sufficient for you, for My strength is made perfect in weakness."
—2 CORINTHIANS 12:9

The sun was shining brightly on that spring afternoon as my three grandsons and I headed to the park for a playdate. Since the time they were babies, I've delighted in interacting with them on the playground equipment. This would be one more memory to add to our treasure trove.

As we approached the playground, my eyes felt as though someone had swished them with acid. I had recently been diagnosed with lupus, an autoimmune disease that basically makes the body allergic to itself. I knew bright lights were one of the problems associated with lupus, and I had worn my sunglasses. But I was devastated as I realized I wouldn't be able to play in the sun with my grandchildren.

They climbed on the play equipment, and I sat down under a shade tree to have an intimate pity party with three familiar friends—me, myself, and I.

Suddenly, I heard singing behind me. "God good.... God good ... all time." I looked around and saw a young man in a wheelchair watching the other kids playing on the equipment.

I assured myself that *he* wasn't singing "God is good ... all the time." Surely not. After all, he could only watch while everyone else had fun.

I kept telling myself that I must have heard the wrong words coming from his lips. Then, my curiosity got the best of me. I turned around and asked, "Son, are you singing, 'God is good.... God is good ... all the time'?"

He nodded his head affirmatively and his uncle, Ray, told me how Isaac certainly was singing those words and that he had also memorized five psalms. Isaac then began reciting Psalm 100:

Make a joyful shout to the LORD, all you lands!
Serve the LORD with gladness;
 Come before His presence with singing.
Know that the LORD, He *is* God;
 It is He *who* has made us, and not we ourselves;
 We are His people and the sheep of His pasture.

Enter into His gates with thanksgiving,

And into His courts with praise.
Be thankful to Him, *and* bless His name.
For the LORD *is* good;
His mercy *is* everlasting,
And His truth *endures* to all generations.

By the time he recited the last verse, I was choking back tears.

"You've been such a blessing to me today, Isaac. I needed to be reminded of God's unchanging goodness, and he put me near you so you could remind me through your life and words. Thank you."

Isaac smiled and then he told me about all the things he *could* do. He was looking forward to riding horses that summer in Washington, D.C., and going to camp in northern Indiana.

Unlike me, Isaac's focus was on the glory and goodness of God. He knew that physical limitations and suffering are God's invitation for us to enter into a more intimate relationship with him.

My grandsons had the privilege of meeting Isaac and Ray, and afterward I explained to them how God made his presence real to me through Isaac. Then, I told them in a simple, nonscary manner why I had new limitations—that I had an illness called lupus that is worse when I'm in sunlight.

I'm not sure how the subject turned from lupus to God, but it did. The four of us discussed heaven. Cole, age six, emphasized that he wanted *only* Jesus in his mansion. I asked if I could visit, and he said yes. We then talked about who we want to meet first when we get there.

Will we sleep? Will there be rules? Will there be cars?

After taking the boys home, my heart felt like a balloon, ready to burst. I may not be able to play in the sun with my grandchildren anymore, but I *can* praise God for his unfailing love under the shade tree of my limitations and for precious talks about Jesus and heaven with my grandsons. What could be better?

I drove home, singing Isaac's simple little words through my tears ... "God is good.... God is good ... *all* the time."

A dipperful of God's grace is always available
for those who need refreshment.

— MICHELLE COX

Dear Lord,
Thank you for the limitations, for they are your invitation
to deeper relationships with you and those I love. Help me
to keep my eyes off my problems and on my problem solver.
Thank you for your presence through the difficult
moments. Help my life to shine for you and help my
actions to remind others that God is good—all the time.
Amen.

TOP 10 MOST ENCOURAGING THINGS ANYONE EVER SAID TO YOU

I love your smile.

You make me happy.

I feel confident knowing you're on my side.

You really listen to me.

I like your style.

You did a fantastic job.

You always make me feel comfortable.

I know I can trust you.

You're the same person inside and out.

Holding your hand is wonderful.

DIVORCE

GOD *Wants* TO FORGIVE US

BARB FAUST

And be kind to one another, tenderhearted, forgiving one another, even as God in Christ forgave you.

—EPHESIANS 4:32

I grew up learning, knowing, believing that divorce was rotten. Degrading. Even though my daughter and I were being abused on a daily basis, I delayed ending my marriage until it became too much to bear.

When we finally left, life became even more humiliating. What had remained hidden was now out in public. Our private heartbreak was fair game for lawyers, judges, police, therapists, social services, family, and friends. Even day-care workers and employers were in the loop because they needed to know about restraining orders.

Finding a church on my own turned into a monumental task. All I wanted was to lean on a few strong shoulders and maybe cry on a couple. What I got was the reminder that unless my ex-spouse married first, I'd be an adulteress. Not exactly the message of comfort for which I'd been hoping.

The pastor, of course, preached against divorce. I expected that. But did he have to tell me he'd never officiate at the ceremony should I decide to remarry? Too much information, much too soon. Sadly, my needs and those of my daughter were ignored.

I'll be honest. I was the only single parent in the congregation, and they didn't know what to do with me. So I kept busy by serving in various capacities. Still the SIN (I always pictured it in all capital letters) of divorce gnawed at me like a starving rat on a hunk of cheese.

For three years the fight continued in court. I filed for divorce and felt that meant I deserved the lion's share of the blame. Would God ever take away the torment of what I had done? Would he ever let me get back to normal? Could he ever *forgive* me?

But then I met Jean. At the time I didn't know that she and her husband had both been divorced. Their marriage together seemed so strong. A beautiful example of how a relationship is supposed to work.

Jean adopted me as her daughter and made my child her granddaughter. Hugs happened often and words of hope were shared regularly. "You're doing a great job as a single parent," Jean would say. That encouragement meant the world to me.

One day she told me something that changed my life forever. Her wisdom helped begin a process of healing for my battered heart. She said, "God's doctrine on forgiveness is greater than his doctrine on divorce."

What? He forgives? Even me? My mind swirled with questions.

"But I thought he hated divorce." I wanted to cling to her words, but were they true?

My dear friend Jean continued. "God *wants* to forgive us of all of our sins. He *wants* to give us peace. God's doctrine on forgiveness *is* greater than his doctrine on divorce. True, he prefers couples to work on their marriage and stay together. But I don't believe God wanted you to stay where you were, living in a situation where you and your daughter were abused."

Could it be? Perhaps I hadn't committed the unforgivable. Maybe divorce didn't have to mean the end of my life, my happiness, or my relationship with Jesus. He still wanted to be my friend no matter what I'd done or thought I'd done.

Jean and I have been friends for years. We've gone through a lot together. The death of her husband, the divorces of two of her children, my own struggles. Loving, caring, and comforting. And always—always—forgiving.

God's forgiveness is a bottomless pool dispensed from his well of grace.

—MICHELLE COX

Dear Lord,
I've experienced your forgiveness on so many occasions.
Thank you for your unlimited mercy and grace. Thank
you for remembering that I'm a flawed human being,
and that despite my failures, my heart longs to please
you. I love you, Lord.
Amen.

DETERMINATION

You're Smart

SUZANNE ALEXANDER—*author and physician*

Ointment and perfume delight the heart, and the sweetness
of a man's friend gives delight by hearty counsel.
—PROVERBS 27:9

I grew up knowing I was dumb, but I sometimes forgot and said smart stuff. No worries though, because Dad was right there to remind me of my flaws by calling me a "dumb Pollock."

One day when I was in the fifth grade, I hurried out the door to walk to school with my friends. I forgot to close the door behind me. Nothing bad happened because the door had been left open. No robber stole our jar of pennies. The dog stayed put.

The only bad thing that happened was Dad yelled. And called me "dumb Pollock" in front of my friends.

I pretended not to care, but secretly wanted to prove my dad wrong. Only I didn't know what "Pollock" meant. Maybe I wasn't too bright.

When we arrived at school, our class got library cards so we could borrow books. I sneaked away to peek at the dictionary. "Pollock," it stated, "was a type of fish." Huh? I ran back to join my class, but couldn't pay attention the rest of the day. Why would Dad call me a fish?

The dumb part I understood.

I dawdled on the way home. My friends were first across the expansive puddle. The tips of my shoes poked over the edge, and I noticed how small my head looked in the reflection.

It dawned on me. My head is small so my brain must be small. Since most fish probably had small brains that must be why Dad called me a dumb fish. Actually, I felt pretty smart for figuring all that out.

Years later, though, I learned he meant something mean and racist which made absolutely no sense. I am not Polish (and neither is he), and the Polish people we knew were pretty smart.

Guess it didn't matter whether or not he meant dumb person or dumb fish. His description became my excuse when I flunked an exam or heard about a school counselor saying I'd better buckle down or I wouldn't amount to a hill of beans.

I was dumb. No question. I hung out with my friends, smoked borrowed cigarettes, and drank cheap liquor.

The truth is my parents had troubles of their own and were doing the best they could. I didn't understand that then. If I had, I might not have felt so blue.

When I was fifteen, we moved to a run-down farmhouse. Our new neighbor was a tiny woman—tiny in size, but not in curiosity. She raised horses, goats, chickens, and five children for good measure. She also pitched in to help her husband run his business.

Since I liked horses, I hung around at her place, picking up what I could. Meanwhile, she was learning everything she could about me. My parents nicknamed her Nosy Neighbor Lady. I didn't care what they called her. She let me ride her horses. Once when she went away on business, she asked me to care for them.

She came back from her trip and looked things over. I wanted everything perfect, so I was nervous. When she finished her inspection, she sat me down.

"You're smart," she said.

I protested. "You've got me all wrong. I'm flunking math and—"

She wouldn't listen. Deep down, I knew she was right. It was scary though, because being smart meant I had far more responsibility than I felt prepared to handle.

Nosy Neighbor Lady wasn't done. She told me I could live a sober and productive life. The idea had never occurred to me before.

I told no one what she had said and avoided her for weeks as I slowly digested her meaty words. Eventually, I visited her farm again. My time with her grew longer and more frequent. Being there made me hope that maybe I could have a future—like her.

One day Nosy Neighbor Lady explained how it wasn't completely my parents' fault that they couldn't shape me into what I was meant to be. Maybe on account of how *they* had been raised. She warned me that if I changed my life they might seem angry at first. It would take them time to understand. That made me feel better.

From that day on, I lost all guilt about listening to her advice. And I prepared for some tough times, believing it would all come together for good in the end. Nosy Neighbor Lady suggested I get serious about school one subject at a time.

That's exactly what I did. And I started getting As.

No one could believe my report card except her. My current friends didn't like the changes they saw so I had to find new ones.

I worked hard, put myself through college, and went on to medical school. Now I am a doctor, wife, and mother. I also play the role of Nosy Neighbor Lady whenever I can, even to my own kids.

And my parents? Now they are so proud of me it's embarrassing.

Not bad for a dumb fish.

The power of our words can brighten the dark places and bring
sunshine and healing to a wounded heart.

—MICHELLE COX

Dear Lord,
Help me to use the power of my words to provide
comfort and healing for those who need to hear them.
Make my life a hospital of hope for those who are
hurting or who need to hear a word of encouragement.
Thank you for your words of comfort that have
sustained me throughout my life.
Amen.

VALUE

PRINCE CHARMING

LEON OVERBAY—*storyteller*

For the LORD does not see as man sees; for man looks at the outward appearance, but the LORD looks at the heart.
—1 SAMUEL 16:7

The year was 1959, and Mrs. Reid was our fifth-grade teacher. She was great. She made profound statements to us children that linger in our minds to this day. She once said, "One third of all the children in the world live in China."

My twin brother and I already knew that the children in China were starving—our parents told us that at the supper table when we didn't clean our plates.

I remember looking around the classroom to try to determine which of the kids in our room lived in China. We knew that one in three lived there. It could have been Katie Johnson. She had a dark complexion, and her eyes were a beautiful almond shape. After Mrs. Reid's statement about

China, we always offered Katie our leftovers in the cafeteria. She thought we were strange.

Mrs. Reid told the class that for the closing program that year, when all the parents came to the PTA, we were going to perform the popular movie of the day, *Snow White and the Seven Dwarfs*. She said there weren't enough acting parts for all the students but she wanted everyone involved.

She immediately appointed four girls as casting directors. She said it was a very important role because they would pick out the actors for the play. She then appointed costume and set designers.

I started thinking about who I would pick if I were a casting director.

Deanna had to be Snow White. She was beautiful, and she looked just like the Snow White in the movies.

Verlin had to be the Woodsman who took Snow White out into the forest. The Woodsman was really big, and Verlin *was* the biggest kid in the class.

Desta had to be the Beautiful Queen who turned into the Evil Hag. Desta was gorgeous, and she had a wart on her nose that would come in handy when she turned into the Evil Hag.

My twin brother, Lynn, had allergies and was sneezing all the time so he should be Sneezy. Everyone knew that Fesser was going to be a doctor so he should be Doc.

Virgil hunted all night and slept through class so he would be Sleepy.

Junior always had a grin on his face so he could be Happy. John didn't want anything to do with the play so he was the perfect pick for Grumpy.

I thought about who I should be in the play. Why, naturally, I should be Prince Charming. It was a given. Who *else* could be Prince Charming? It *had* to be me.

I began showing off to the girls who were casting directors. I posed and flexed my muscles. I showed them my profile while flashing a big smile. I made sure I was always in front of them so they would know that I should be Prince Charming.

The day finally came when Mrs. Reid would announce the parts for the play. The first one chosen was Deanna, for the part of Snow White. That one was a given.

The next part chosen was that of the Woodsman. Just as expected, they chose big ol' Verlin.

They then called on Desta to be the Beautiful Queen who turned into the Evil Hag. That was a natural choice. Remember, she *was* beautiful … and there was the wart thing.

Mrs. Reid then called up my twin brother and announced the part of Sneezy. Yep, those allergies had won him the role.

Just as expected, they gave the part of Doc to Fesser, then called up Junior and gave him the part of Happy. And John got the part of Grumpy. Naturally, they got the parts. Junior had a big grin on his face, and John had a big frown.

They then called me to the front of the room. There were just a couple of parts left and one of them was Prince Charming. There was *no way* anyone else could be Prince Charming.

Mrs. Reid announced to the class that the casting directors were unanimous in this decision. They said I wouldn't even have to act. I just had to be myself. I waited expectantly. Mrs. Reid then announced to the class, "Leon, you have the part of … Dopey."

Those words crushed me. You think you are Prince Charming, but others think you're Dopey.

I now have a granddaughter named Allison. Last year she was in kindergarten. My wife keeps her after school at our house until her parents pick her up.

Sometimes I slip out of work early to come home and spend time with her. She calls me Buddy. On this particular day, she said, "Buddy, will you watch a movie with me?"

"Sure, Allison." We went into the living room, and she loaded a cassette into the VCR. When *Snow White and the Seven Dwarfs* popped onto the screen, I realized it was the same movie that we'd performed when I was in the fifth grade.

I put my arm around Allison so she wouldn't be scared when the Beautiful Queen turned into the Evil Hag. Allison had seen the movie several times, and she sang the parts of Snow White. She was impressed with me when I sang along with the Dwarf parts.

When the movie was over, I asked Allison, "If we were going to cast parts for this, what part would you be?"

She replied, "Well, of course, Buddy, I would be Snow White."

"Allison, what part do you think I would be?"

She said, "Well, of course, Buddy, you would be Prince Charming."

It took me nearly fifty years, but I finally got the part.

Her simple words were a reminder that what we say can change a life. Sometimes others beat people down, and they end up feeling like they're Dopey. They take on that role when they might really be Prince Charming—if only someone will tell them that they are.

Looking back, none of the girls that were casting directors for my fifth-grade play ever went on to become one in real life. I believe one day, however, you will see on the credits of a major motion picture "Allison Overbay—Casting Director."

We gaze in the mirror and focus on our flaws,
but when God looks at us through his mirror
of grace, he just notices his beloved child.

—MICHELLE COX

Dear Lord,

Thank you for loving me in spite of my flaws and failures. When I'm discouraged, remind me that I'm of value to you. Make me an encourager. Help me to look at others through your eyes and use my words to remind them that they are of such value to you that you gave your precious son for them.

Amen.

ABILITY

GOD'S PLANS

LISA SMITH—*sign-language signer with Sandi Patty, Women of Faith, and others*—AS TOLD BY VICKI SMITH TO MICHELLE COX

I will praise You, for I am fearfully and wonderfully made.
—PSALM 139:14

The mood at the Bobcat Arena in Charlotte, North Carolina, was electrifying as the packed house worshipped God at the Women of Faith conference. The music group Avalon walked onstage, joined by a young woman named Lisa Smith who would sign the songs as they sang.

I was perched in the top section, my high vantage point giving an antlike quality to the performers below. As the music filled the center, Lisa signed, literally bouncing with enthusiasm. I turned to my friend, "Now *that's* the joy of the Lord."

She quietly replied, "Did you see her face? She has Down syndrome."

I looked at the giant monitors in the middle of the convention hall. Yes, the telltale features were there, but they were overshadowed by Lisa's love for the Lord lighting her face with a glowing smile.

Tears filled my eyes as she enthusiastically signed words about God's goodness and faithfulness. Lisa appeared to be about thirty years old, and as I watched her that day, I couldn't help but wonder what her parents had been told when she was born....

The year was 1975, and Vicki was breathing a sigh of relief as she reached the end of her pregnancy. After three miscarriages, the normalcy of this pregnancy had been a blessing.

The big day finally came, and Vicki went into labor. When she arrived at the hospital, the medical personnel strapped a fetal heart monitor on her. Sometime later, she realized she didn't hear the baby's heartbeat. The doctor immediately prepped her and then performed an emergency C-section.

The anesthesia knocked Vicki for a loop. When she finally started coming to, her first question was, "Is the baby okay?"

Her husband replied quietly, "The doctors aren't saying she's retarded, but they said she might be slow."

"What does that mean?"

"I'm not really sure."

As the day progressed, they were puzzled by the strange behavior of the medical staff. Everyone seemed to avoid them.

The nurses would bring the baby to the other mom in the semi-private room, and they would laugh and talk with her. When they brought Lisa, they just placed her in Vicki's arms without saying a word and then turned and left.

Vicki was almost ready to leave the hospital when a doctor came to her room. "Are you sure you want to take this baby home with you?"

Vicki was puzzled. "What do you mean? I'm not leaving this hospital *without* her."

She returned a week later to have her stitches removed. Again, the medical staff seemed to avoid her. Vicki asked, "Doctor, why is everyone acting so strange?"

"We think the baby might be a mongoloid."

Vicki was stunned. "She looks normal to me. Why would you think she's a mongoloid?"

"Well, there are some indicators—she has a curved baby finger, there's extra fatty tissue behind her neck, and her eyes are slanted. When she's four weeks old, we'll do a chromosome test at Albany Medical. You should hear the results about four weeks after that."

Vicki had eight weeks to bond with her baby girl, to absorb her sweetness, to snuggle her close and kiss her tiny toes. Eight weeks to fall head over heels in love with this tiny child God had entrusted to her.

At the end of the two months, the phone rang and the voice

on the other end said, "The results are back. Your baby *does* have Down syndrome."

She remembers thanking them. What else could she say? Then she told her husband and they cried together, their hearts aching at what the diagnosis would mean to the little one who had stolen their hearts. Both verbalized the same thought, "It doesn't matter. This is a baby who needs our love."

Vicki began reading everything she could about the disorder. She'd received a twelve-month magazine subscription during her pregnancy. Each issue featured segments on baby growth and development.

And that's when a mother's fierce love began making a difference. A few months ahead of the scheduled development, Vicki started working with Lisa on each skill.

Determined that her child would have every chance, she took her for physical and occupational therapy. The results were amazing. By fifteen months, Lisa had a fifteen-word vocabulary, and the only area where she lagged behind was that she was slow in walking.

During her first eighteen months, Lisa had pneumonia four times. The family moved from New York to Dallas, hoping that the change in climate would help. A few months after the move, Lisa's sister, Lori, was born, providing Lisa with a playmate and a role model to mimic.

Vicki and the girls began attending Royal Haven Baptist

Church. A few months later, Vicki walked down the aisle, accepting Jesus as her Savior, meeting the God who became her strength, provision, and comfort.

And God did provide for their needs as he sent people into Lisa's life who would nurture and challenge her to reach her potential.

At a Sunday-morning worship service in July 2000, Lisa was singing her heart out and signing with what little sign language she knew. An elderly couple sitting nearby wept as they observed her uninhibited love for the Lord.

The incident caused Vicki to wonder if Lisa might enjoy signing to music, so she asked her friend Marla, a high school sign-language teacher, if she would teach her daughter how to sign just one song.

Marla told Lisa to choose a song, and then she began teaching her the chorus. She showed her how to write out the words, look up the corresponding sign in the American Sign Language Book, and write down the page number over the word.

Marla was going to be away for two weeks, so she told Lisa to practice while she was gone. Lisa learned the chorus in two days. She was eager to learn more, so she and Vicki worked on the rest of the lyrics. By the end of the two weeks, Lisa had learned the entire song.

Vicki wanted to make sure Lisa was learning correctly, so she called Marla and asked for a time when Lisa could perform the song for her. Marla was stunned as she watched. "Vicki, you don't understand. This is a gift from God. I have had students in my class for more than a year who never learned one song."

Lisa performed one evening when friends were over for dinner. Their hearts were moved as they watched her. "She needs to do this for the Women's Bible Study."

They made arrangements, and she signed for seven hundred women, receiving her first standing ovation and an invitation to sign for fifteen hundred people at the Sunday worship service. Her joy-filled performance made the words of the song come alive.

Lisa's hero was Sandi Patty, and one day she told her mom, "I'm going to sign with her."

Trying to let her down easy—believing it would never happen—Vicki replied, "Lisa, just pray about it. Sandi's a famous singer, and she can't perform with everyone who would like to sing with her."

A few years later, Vicki and Lisa were sitting in the second row at a Sandi Patty concert. A mutual acquaintance had e-mailed Sandi about Lisa, and halfway through the concert, she motioned for Lisa to come on stage with her.

Lisa was beyond excited. Sandi asked if Lisa knew two songs. By now, she had learned 125, and most of them were Sandi's songs.

Sandi took center stage, and the two worshipped God in

tandem, Sandi's glorious voice filling the concert hall, and Lisa's heartfelt performance filling the hearts of all who watched.

Since that day, Lisa has performed with Sandi Patty on many occasions, including on international television. She's signed with Avalon, Larnelle Harris, Kathy Troccoli, Bebe Winans, and she's signed at numerous Women of Faith conferences.

In 1975, the doctors said, "Put her in an institution. She'll never amount to anything."

In 2006, I sat in the crowd at a Women of Faith conference, and I could almost hear God reply, "Not *this* child. I have plans for her. I'm going to put her on a platform and let her sparkle for me. I'm going to let her contagious joy touch the hearts of thousands as her hands sign words of praise for me."

And that's exactly what God did.

Our worst disability occurs when we don't use our
ability and availability for God.

— MICHELLE COX

Dear Lord,
Thank you for your faithfulness. I'm grateful
that you're bigger than all of my problems and that
nothing comes as a surprise to you. Remind
me to trust in you when I'm faced with difficult
situations, knowing that you are sufficient
for my every need. Help me to live my life in a
manner that will bring glory to you.
Amen.

LOVE

JUST LOVING MY HUSBAND

DIANE REILLY

The heart of her husband safely trusts her;
so he will have no lack of gain.
—PROVERBS 31:11

We had been away from home, and upon our return I called a dear friend to catch up on the latest news. When I asked how she had been spending her time, she replied, "I've just been loving my husband."

My initial reaction was to think *and what else?* As time went by though, I kept feeling that gentle nudging in my heart that though I was doing many good things, I was certainly *not* loving my husband, Bob, as I should be loving him.

I was so busy with my list of things to do that I looked for ways to keep my retired husband occupied elsewhere so I could get the important things done.

I'd always told people that God was first in my life and then my next priority was my husband. But was it? God began to show me many little ways that I could respect him, meeting his needs and truly honoring him.

I began to show interest in the book he was reading, and asking if there was a movie he wanted to see or anything else he wanted to do.

And I changed some habits like sighing when he'd forget something, listening halfheartedly when he'd make a request, or responding negatively when his dirty laundry didn't get tossed into the hamper.

I've read in the Bible that we can't love God any more than we love our husbands, and I have found that after forty-two years of marriage, I still have much to learn.

I've been making Bob my real priority and have watched him relax, seen his joy return, and watched anxieties disappear as we pray together.

I'm learning to speak his love languages of touch and words of encouragement. Everything on my list is falling into place, and the next time someone asks me what I've been doing, I'll tell them, "I've just been loving my husband."

Ironically, our trip away was to visit an old roommate of Bob's who was terminally ill with a brain tumor. It made us all realize that each day together is a tremendous gift. What we do with that day is our gift to others—and to God. I plan to spend the rest of my days enjoying the gift of "loving my husband."

The funny thing about love is that every time you give it away,
it boomerangs back to you.

—MICHELLE COX

Dear Lord,
Thank you for this special person you have placed in my
life. Let my actions be an extension of your loving-
kindness for me. Give me joy as I care for my spouse
and our home and help my words to bring
encouragement that will color each day with love.
Amen.

THE PHONE CALL OF ENCOURAGEMENT

The phone call is quick and easy and often lots of fun. But because of busy schedules, be prepared to leave your message with the answering machine. The phone call of encouragement is an excellent way to tell someone how much you care—to let them know you're thinking and praying for them. Remember, though, they can hear your voice. When encouraging someone, let them hear the smile in your tone. Keep such calls light and hopeful. And if the situation merits, let them know what you'd like to do to help. Perhaps prepare a meal, pick up some groceries, or watch their children for an afternoon. Or stop by with flowers. Mean what you say and follow through. In that way you can help shoulder a heavy burden for the person on the other end of the line.

COUNSEL

GOD WILL HONOR YOUR SACRIFICE

CARLTON HUGHES—*professor and children's pastor*

Listen to counsel and receive instruction,
that you may be wise in your latter days.
—PROVERBS 19:20

The voice on the other end of the phone squealed in delight. "Mr. Hughes! Carlton Hughes! This is too weird—I was just talking about you yesterday."

I had called Haley, a former student from the community college where I teach, to schedule her as a chapel speaker at my sons' Christian school. Now I was curious as to why she had been talking about me.

"I was speaking to a friend of mine about a tough decision she had just made," Haley said. "I shared with her the advice you gave me."

Advice? I didn't remember giving Haley advice.

Peppy and full of life, Haley had arrived at our rural community college from the "big city," eager to escape the pressures of urban life and to finish her education in a more peaceful setting. She'd moved in with her grandmother and aunt, who had started taking her to church.

Since she was attending church on a regular basis, Haley assumed that she was automatically a Christian, so she joined the Christian students' club that I helped sponsor.

We didn't judge her or try to convert her—we just loved her. She proved to be quite a seeker, hungry to learn more about God. She eventually accepted Christ, and her fellow students and I rejoiced.

Shortly after that, she started dating a nice Christian guy, and they eventually married. They finished their degrees to be teachers—Haley in elementary education, her husband in secondary; and both found work in the local school system.

I had seen her periodically over the years since her graduation, mostly brief encounters at the shopping center.

Haley was a determined, strong-willed young lady. I certainly didn't recall giving *her* any life-changing advice.

"What advice?" I asked.

She reminded me that the last time we had met, she had just given birth to a daughter and was contemplating quitting her job to become a stay-at-home mom. She had fallen madly in love with her darling baby and couldn't imagine anyone else taking care of her.

Still, she was a bit apprehensive about her decision, which would mean leaving behind half of the family's income, not to mention her tenure-track position.

"That's when you said those words that changed my life."

What words?

"You told me 'God will honor your sacrifice,'" she said, "and I have held onto those words ever since."

Wow. Had I really said that?

The conversation started coming back to me. I had shared with Haley that after our two sons were born, my wife and I decided it was best for her to stay home. I had told Haley that it hadn't been completely easy for us—my family certainly had our share of struggles with finances and with other things, but that God had honored our sacrifice for our children.

When the time was right and our sons were both in school full time, God opened a door for my wife to work at their school—the perfect position at just the right time—a job where she could use her gifts and abilities like never before and still be close to our children.

And yes, now I did vaguely remember closing that long-ago encounter with those simple words, "God will honor your sacrifice."

Haley shared that a friend of hers had recently left a secure position in the city to come to our rural area to serve, and that like Haley, this friend was having second thoughts about her decision. Haley had shared my words, and the message had brought comfort to her friend.

At this point in the conversation, Haley began thanking me profusely for those words of wisdom—words I barely remembered saying.

I thanked her for being so kind and then scheduled her to speak at a chapel service. I knew she and her husband had been active volunteers with the youth group at their church for years; plus I remembered she had the gift of gab, so I was excited that I'd get to hear her speak.

When I hung up the phone, I experienced a different kind of excitement, the trembling kind. I was overwhelmed with the fact that God had actually used my words to touch someone—who in turn blessed another life.

What an awesome miracle—and what an awesome responsibility. How many times had I been careless with words? How many times had I said things in jest, words that might have brought hurt instead of healing?

I went to the Lord in prayer, thanking him for using me, repenting of any words I had said that hurt someone, and asking for his help in sharing more words of hope and healing.

Good counsel has no price.

—GIUSEPPE MAZZINI

Dear Lord,

Thank you for those who gave wise counsel when I needed it. Give me wisdom to help those around me as they seek to live their lives for you. Guard my tongue from speaking careless words that hurt instead of heal. Help my words to be a blessing to others.

Amen.

WELCOME

JANE ARDELEAN

Show mercy and compassion
Everyone to his brother.
—ZECHARIAH 7:9

It was hard to believe this was the last day of my teaching career. I thought of my thirty-four years spent in Christian, missionary, and now public schools. My current crop of fourth graders, as well as former students, came to my classroom to wish me well. They showered me with flowers, candy, a quilt, and many warm hugs.

Sadness hung heavily as I looked at the last report card on my desk. All of the other children had come early to pick up their final grades. Except for Tyler.

At the beginning of the school year, my principal asked if Tyler could join my class for one hour each morning. His special-education teachers wanted to try to mainstream this autistic child so he could experience the camaraderie of a regular classroom. I agreed. "We'll give him a warm welcome."

The principal warned, "The boy can't stand having anyone touch him." Since birth, he abhorred such attention. Any contact made him growl. After my students came in, I told them about the new student joining us the next day. I explained that Tyler might feel nervous.

I had an idea. "How about making him a special card since tomorrow is his birthday?" Tyler, like so many youngsters, was obsessed with Star Wars.

The children drew pictures, and I bought a toy. We piled them on Tyler's desk. I also made it clear that no one should touch Tyler because that bothered him. "Be very kind to him. Let's make him feel welcome." I encouraged them to set an example for others. They took my words to heart.

Large for his age, Tyler came in with his father. He shuffled in, seeing only strangers.

"Welcome to class," I said. When he saw his desk piled high with Star Wars cards and toys, he examined his treasures and cautiously sat down.

As the days passed, I came to admire Tyler's wonderfully creative block structures. One day I patted him on the back and said, "Great job, Tyler!"

I was startled at my boldness. Would he growl at me? Fortunately, he didn't make even a tentative grunt. As he grew more comfortable, he would sometimes blurt out a word or two.

He felt welcome. He felt safe. Partly because two boys became his protectors and friends. As he left for art or music, the pair walked beside Tyler like secret-service agents. Truth was he'd taught the entire class something.

And now on this last day of my last year, a lone report card remained unclaimed. Perhaps the staff would have to mail it.

I wanted to say good-bye to Tyler. But he wasn't coming.

Everything was packed, and I needed to lock up my room for the last time. "Look who's here!" I heard the deep voice of Tyler's father. His son stood by his side at my doorway.

I looked at the man. "Having Tyler here was a privilege." Turning to the boy I said, "Did you have a good year?"

A strong "Uh-huh" issued as he nodded his head.

"Tyler, could I have a hug?" I held my breath and waited. Very slowly Tyler spread his arms and gave me a bear hug.

And all the way home, I heard God's encouraging words: "Good job, Jane. That hug was from me."

A warm welcome is first cooked up in the heart.

—MICHELLE COX

Dear Lord,

I'm grateful that your welcome mat is always out. Remind me that there are people all around me who are hurting, who are lonely, and who feel unloved. Help me to share your love and compassion with those who need to hear the words "You are welcome here."

Amen.

THE SMILE OF ENCOURAGEMENT

Anyone can succeed at this! If you're uncomfortable with hugs or handshakes, use your smile to let someone know that you're listening … and that you care. But keep it real. A phony face glows like neon. If you don't know exactly what to do or what to say, let your friend talk. And listen carefully, praying as you do. If there's something practical you can do or say to encourage him or her, go where the Lord leads. Smiling all the way. You might even want to lean over and share a warm embrace. Again, keep the focus on the person you hope to encourage. Make sure they're comfortable and that you're allowing for personal space. Be sure, too, that you're not wearing out your welcome. Lighten someone's load by your smile … and by other simple gestures of encouragement.

INSPIRATION

GOD LOVES YOU

VIRGINIA CHATMAN

God is love, and he who abides
in love abides in God, and God in him.
—1 JOHN 4:16

I grew up in Miami, Florida. When I was sixteen, I began to look earnestly for answers to tough questions. My mother once said the most powerful book in the world was the Bible. So I decided to look there first.

Why was I alive? What would happen to me when I died?

For some reason, I started in Job. It depressed me so much that I opened up the book of John instead. A miracle happened.

The words changed me. My mind was totally transformed when I realized Jesus was the only answer for life's questions. I knelt beside my bed and accepted him as Savior.

In my twenties, my pastor challenged me to surrender my

life to Christ. And the only way to know him was to know the Bible. His statements moved me to action.

I grasped very little about the Bible but wanted to be closer to Christ. My prayers centered on seeking God's will and then following through. Doing what he wanted me to do.

In time I enrolled at Miami Bible College. My sole objective was to know Christ as revealed in Scripture.

My schedule consisted of school in the mornings and work in the afternoons in downtown Miami. Though busy, I had a joy in my heart because of what I was learning. But as happens to every believer, I grew weary.

I couldn't help wondering, "Jesus, do you love me?"

The question haunted me. How could I even have such a thought? I reminded myself of the cross and all he had done for me. It helped but wasn't enough.

Finally, I cried out to him, "Please, just say to me, 'I love you.'" I needed to—wanted to—hear those words. I listened in silence.

During my time at college, I often rode the bus. To reach my workplace, I had to take two buses. Transferring at one location was quite safe, but my next option was a dangerous part of the city. So I always skipped that stop. I never felt comfortable seeing the weary, desperate faces.

One day I was befuddled and got off at the wrong place. Fear gripped me, and I prayed for God's protection. I knew numerous murders had been committed in this area. Alone in the crowd, I quickly claimed a bus bench and waited. "Please, God, make me invisible."

I prayed no one would notice me or even sit near. I got my answer immediately when a filthy bum settled in. He was stubbly, scruffy, and he smelled.

My next prayer, of course, was that he would not speak to me. Just leave me in peace.

As this plea wafted heavenward, he began talking to me. Wouldn't leave me alone. I didn't want to be rude, but I had no desire to speak to him. I refused to let him see my fright.

But he wouldn't be ignored. Finally, he turned to me and said, "There is something God wants to tell you."

What in the world would this man say next? I waited, curious.

"God wants you to know that he loves you."

"What did you say?" I heard but couldn't believe.

"God loves you." He spoke clearly—to me.

Whether man or angel, his words were a gift. Before I could thank him, the bus appeared. Trembling, I hurried on board.

God's messenger had met me. Given me the peace I longed to hear in a place where I felt most alone. Most frightened.

I am retired now. My life has been full of examples of God's faithfulness. Sometimes when friends express fears about tomorrow, I'm tempted to join in the worry session.

Then I think about that scruffy man at the bus stop. And I remember the God who's in charge.

The love of God is broader than the measure of man's mind.

—FREDERICK W. FABER

> *Dear Lord,*
> *I'm grateful that you're an on-time God. You know my needs, and you always supply just what I need exactly when I need it. Thank you for your peace and your faithfulness. I'm glad you're in charge of every aspect of my life.*
> *Amen.*

GRATITUDE

COUNTING MY BLESSINGS

MICHELLE COX

I will make them and the places all around My hill a
blessing; and I will cause showers to come down in their
season; there shall be showers of blessing.

—EZEKIEL 34:26

My husband and I had enjoyed working with the singles' ministry at Trinity Baptist Church for several years. We were thrilled when the opportunity arose to take the group on a mission trip to Costa Rica.

After months of fundraising and preparation, everyone was excited when the plane finally touched down in San Jose.

The ride from the airport to the mission house brought much laughter as the group observed the anything-goes traffic with horns blowing, cars darting in and out in a crazy manner, and bicyclists riding in the middle of the chaos.

Our bus left the busy city and drove into smaller neighborhoods where the houses were surrounded by tall walls topped with barbed wire. Over the next few days, other cultural differences became apparent as the group ate beans and rice at every meal (including breakfast!), and sampled unfamiliar fruits and vegetables.

Our hosts had planned the week carefully, providing a nice balance of work and sightseeing. We "oohed" and "aahed" as we traveled through the lush beauty of the rain forest, visited a coffee plantation, and witnessed the Arenal Volcano erupt against the background of the night sky.

The journey throughout Costa Rica revealed a country with spectacular waterfalls and vivid tropical flowers. On our riverboat ride at Rio Sarapiqui, we observed crocodiles sunning on the banks of the rivers and monkeys chattering as they swung from tree to tree.

A visit to a mountaintop restaurant provided a panoramic view of the nighttime lights of San Jose—and a visual reminder of the millions of people awaiting the light of the gospel.

By the end of the week, our team had poured a concrete slab for an Awana ministry, installed lights and ceiling fans for a church, painted Sunday-school rooms, and built benches for church services.

And we had fallen in love with the Costa Rican people, especially the children with their beautiful eyes and shy smiles.

Our group experienced many heart-tugging moments. One occurred during a nursing-home visit where we met an elderly patient whose husband had locked her in a closet for many years. Malnutrition had left her body the size of a small child.

We cried at the orphanage as we performed a puppet show and

handed out toys to those precious children who had no mothers or fathers, no one to hug them or to dry their tears when they were hurt.

Our final project for the week was to build a small metal house for a Nicaraguan refugee family who had lost their home in a mudslide. Some of the men left early that morning to set things up for our work crew. The rest of us filled plastic bags with dry cereal to give to the children in the neighborhood and then packed a cooler with supplies for lunch.

Laughter and the buzz of conversation filled the bus as we drove to our destination. Our first glimpse of the poverty-stricken community brought instant silence to the group. None of us had ever experienced anything like this before.

A dirty, trash-filled stream trickled down the mountainside. Hundreds of tiny shacks haphazardly dotted the hillside, each a patchwork of cast-off building materials, old signs, and rusting metal. The humidity of the day intensified the unpleasant aromas.

The new home's building site was adjacent to the shanty where the Garcia family was currently living. I saw my husband carrying building materials, and as I walked up to him, I realized he was crying.

"See that little boy over there? He … doesn't have any shoes. There's no plumbing, and he's walking in sewage-contaminated soil. Go look inside where the family is living now."

The shack was constructed of wooden pallets and scraps of metal, and the floor was packed dirt. There were gaping holes in the walls and when it rained, the water flooded in on all sides.

Their worldly possessions consisted of a few tattered chairs, an ancient crib, and a scarred table. The family ate in shifts because they didn't own enough dishes for all the family members to eat at once.

We realized how little the family had—and how much *we* had taken for granted.

Several of us prepared sandwiches, and the team gathered for lunch in the tiny home. Carlos Garcia thanked everyone for coming to help them. And then, standing there in the middle of dirt floors and poverty, he said the words that I'll never forget. "God, I thank you for how you've blessed my family. You've been so good to us."

His sincere prayer touched every heart in the room. I heard sniffles all around me. You see, this man who had so little had discovered something that most of us had failed to remember— that little is much when God is in it. He realized he was rich because he had God in his life.

The team worked with renewed effort that afternoon, determined that the family would have a waterproof home before we departed from Costa Rica.

When we left the work site that evening, we couldn't wait to go shopping. We arrived at the import store, and the minute the bus doors opened, the singles streamed into the building like workers on a busy anthill.

Shopping carts were soon piled high with towels and dishes, pots and pans, and sheets for the new bunk beds we had built. We shopped until we couldn't think of one more thing that the family might need.

Faces beamed with joyous excitement as everyone emptied their billfolds and talked about the surprise for the Garcia family.

The next day when the house was completed, we showered the family with love and gifts—including enough dishes for everyone to eat at once. I don't think any of us ever had more fun.

We went to Costa Rica expecting to touch lives. Instead, *our* lives were changed. You see, we came home counting our blessings, with that dear man's words ringing in our ears and embedded in our hearts, "God, I thank you for how you've blessed my family. You've been so good to us." And indeed, he has.

Our days would be much different
if we changed our attitude to gratitude.

—MICHELLE COX

Dear Lord,
Thank you for blessing my life so abundantly. Give me a
grateful spirit and a heart of compassion that will nurture
others. Thank you for your faithfulness. I thank you for
how you've blessed my family. You've been so good to us.
Amen.

TOP 10 THINGS YOU SHOULD SAY TO YOUR CHILDREN

I love you.

You are a treasure from God.

I'm glad you were born.

Try it ... you can do anything!

I believe in you.

You make me smile.

Don't worry ... I'm always here for you.

I'm glad you're my friend.

Jesus loves you.

I'm praying for you.

PROVISION

That's Papaw's Baby

Sharon E. Carrns—*author*

And my God shall supply all your need according to
His riches in glory by Christ Jesus.
—Philippians 4:19

I was six years old when my father took his life. There were few good memories in my short time with him, and I grew up without any example of what it was like to have a father.

Dad came home an alcoholic after the Korean War, and he never spent more than a three-month stretch out of a veteran's hospital.

Money was always tight, and moves were all too frequent. Sometimes we would take our things with us. Sometimes we would leave them behind.

My mother could not always carry the load of my brother and me alone, though she worked full time to pay the bills.

At times, she suffered with asthma. During one of her hospital stays, my father, in a drunken state, decided to take me to the door of a stranger's house. He said, "My wife is in the hospital, and I can't take care of this baby anymore."

The couple called the hospital and explained the situation, inquiring if they might have a patient with a blonde-haired baby girl. They found my mom, and she called Grammy and Papaw. And I went home to the one place that represented security to me—the farm.

Over the years, my mother would often drive a couple of hours north to take my brother and me to my grandparents' farm in northern Wisconsin so they could care for us. The big old farmhouse provided warmth and safety for me—safe like my Grammy's arms and the foldout couch next to the kitchen.

In the early hours as the sun lit the kitchen, my Grammy lit the gas stove to start breakfast while Papaw finished the chores in the barn. The strong smell of the sulfur match would mingle with the aromas of crackling bacon and hot buttermilk biscuits, and I would awaken to a morning filled with love and security.

Papaw would tromp up the steps, the screen door slamming as he hurried in, and then he would wash up to eat. He'd be laughing most of the time, making up some silly song with lyrics that made us laugh.

I'd climb eagerly onto his lap, and he would throw his head back, joyfully exclaiming, "That's Papaw's baby!" Then he would rub me with his whiskers. I'd nuzzle in for a torrent of tickling and mad kisses on my neck.

When we were a little older, we would spend entire summers on Papaw's farm. Every time I returned, the feeling of being loved and cherished surrounded me like a warm embrace.

That dear man who acted as a father figure to me in my childhood years had built the foundation. He had been God's provision for me until my mom married the man that became my dad.

Grown-up life arrived, and with it came a broken engagement, a broken marriage, and a broken woman. When the hardest times hit, I headed home for the security of the farm.

You see, even with the many wounds from my tattered childhood, deep inside my heart, a voice spoke words that reminded me there was a beauty in me worth loving.

Counselors say that it is difficult to imagine a loving God if you have not experienced a loving human father. When the day came that I was introduced to my heavenly Father, I could believe I was his baby, loved and cherished—broken but able to heal—because I had first been Papaw's baby.

What an awesome responsibility to be
the human representative of a heavenly Father.
—MICHELLE COX

Dear Lord,
Guide my days as a father. Let my child see you in me.
Help me to provide a loving and secure environment for
this little life that you've entrusted to me. Remind me
that my words can wound or they can encourage.
Amen.

LEADERSHIP

A Chip Off the "Andy" Block

Pat Gelsinger—*senior vice president of Intel Corporation*

Hear instruction and be wise, and do not disdain it.
—Proverbs 8:33

In 1985, at a late stage in the development of the 80386 microprocessor for Intel, I gave a presentation to upper-level management. I had gone from being a technician to an engineer but was still quite junior.

I managed a few technicians, gaining credibility and increasingly responsible roles within the design team. However, most of the upper management didn't know me. I had made it past private first class, but not too much further in my career progression.

At this time, I was directly in charge of the tapeout process for the 80386. Tapeout is the very last step of a four-to-five-year development process after which the first design is sent into manufacturing to see if all those transistors we've been laboring on for many years will, by good fortune and much preparation and innovation, actually work as envisioned.

The point of my presentation was that, because of serious, persistent problems with our computer systems, disaster loomed on the horizon. We might never be able to finish the chip. This created a buzz of controversy, but I stood by my data and assertion and insisted that we urgently escalate the matter with our mainframe supplier to get the issues resolved.

One day a week or so after this meeting, I was huddled comfortably in my office, intently working on a portion of the chip. Wrapped in my own little world of problems, ideas, and design, it might have taken a cannon blast to bring me back to the surrounding environment. Instead, all it took was a phone ring.

I had absolutely no desire to be disturbed and was annoyed at this blast of bells. After several rings, which didn't stop despite my reluctance to answer, I picked up the phone and in the most irritated and sarcastic voice I could muster, I demanded, "Who is it?"

"Andy," came the baritone response.

To which I, attempting to outdo the sarcasm of my greeting, bellowed "Andy *who*?"

The response came back quickly, "Andy Grove."

I almost died. This was none other than *the* Andy Grove—a

refugee from Hungary who arrived in the United States with nothing and rose to become an icon of the high-tech industry. One of the founders of the company and now president. Destined to become CEO, then chairman. Later named Time Magazine Man of the Year. Known for his tough, penetrating questions. One of the most well-known, honored, and feared individuals of the entire high-tech community. He was probably ten layers above me, a virtual unknown at Intel. And now he was calling me!

I was more embarrassed than any other time I can recall. Andy seemed undeterred, however, and he described how my presentation the other day had impressed him. He wanted to know my career plans at the company.

After a weak reply, he began shelling me with rapid-fire questions, "What are your goals? What do you read? What are you studying? What do you want to be your next job?"

Flustered, I could barely form adequate sentences in response—much less a substantive answer to his rapid questions.

Following a few of his pointed questions and my weak responses, Andy replied, "Those are lousy answers. Be in my office within two weeks with better ones."

He was right about my answers. I had been startled by his call and entirely unprepared for his line of questioning. Besides, other than "being an engineer," I hadn't given careful consideration to what I wanted to accomplish.

I scheduled an appointment in a couple of weeks and went with trepidation to Andy's office to discuss my career and development goals. This began an ad hoc mentoring relationship that continues to this day, where he is now partially retired and serving as an advisor to Intel; and I'm a senior vice president for the company.

As he would see weaknesses or problems in my character, or as I would struggle with certain areas or issues, I'd get some time on his calendar, and he would offer his wealth of experience, genius, and expertise to this young, ambitious soul. Among other things, he encouraged me to broaden my reading interests and sharpen my career goals.

I still reflect on this experience and say, "Wow!" Andy reached numerous layers down in the organization and tapped me on the shoulder. As president of the company, he was incredibly busy with other aspiring and capable individuals surrounding him.

He humbled me, but his interest in my career also motivated me. I listened studiously to his guidance. I might question his comments but never would I dismiss them. His words that day, "What are your goals?" unquestionably changed the course of my career and life.

Good leadership consists in showing average people
how to do the work of superior people.

—JOHN D. ROCKEFELLER

Dear Lord,
Help me to be a leader who will lead others to you.
Make me a man or woman of character and integrity.
Give me a heart that's willing to live your plan for my
life. Let my words be used to encourage and challenge
others to be their best.
Amen.

A DAILY PRACTICE

S. TRUETT CATHY—*founder and CEO of Chick-fil-A*

While attending high school, I took a course titled "Everyday Living." The teacher's name was Mr. Dean Dyer, and he presented the book *Think and Grow Rich* by Napoleon Hill. This book, along with the teachings of Mr. Dyer, instilled in me the security and confidence to believe in myself. I needed the encouragement.

Everyone should practice encouragement daily. Through Mr. Dyer's direction, I found that I could turn a terrific amount of "want to" into action and enjoy the great benefit of achievement.

"But exhort one another daily, while it is called 'Today'" (Hebrews 3:13).

ENCOURAGEMENT

AVERY'S NEW SHOES

LEON OVERBAY—*storyteller*

*A man who has friends must himself be friendly, but there
is a friend who sticks closer than a brother.*
—PROVERBS 18:24

The year was 1959, and baseball was the national pastime. On Sunday afternoons, a bunch of boys and a few girls would gather in the pasture behind the Gillen's. We ranged in age from about eight to fifteen, and there were usually enough players for two full teams.

Since my dad coached the local Little League team, we kept the equipment at our house; so bats, baseballs, and catcher's equipment were always available.

We'd played so often that we had it down to a science. The two biggest kids in attendance would throw the bat in the air then grab it, placing hand over hand until there was no bat left. The winner would pick first.

The two captains would choose, one after the other, until everyone was on a team. The one who chose first would be the home team and bat last.

The batting order was decided by the position played. The pitcher batted first, then the catcher, then first base, second base, and so on.

The pitchers would always have mercy on the smallest and least experienced, even to the point of pitching underhanded. Sometimes we didn't count outs and batted until everyone had a chance at bat, then we switched sides. None of us had any hostility. We counted hitting the ball into the creek as an automatic home run.

We mowed the infield with a push mower but let the outfield grass grow. The tall grass would slow the ball down before it went into the creek. Yes, there were cow piles everywhere, but we were country kids. No one even noticed.

Eddie was the biggest and the oldest and the toughest. No one was crazy enough to mess with him, but he was also kindhearted and wouldn't do anything to hurt anyone.

On this particular day, Eddie was playing center field and Avery was playing left. My brother hit a long fly ball that ended up over Avery's head in the middle of the creek.

Avery stood on the bank, looking in the creek for the ball. Eddie came up behind him. The day was hot. And Eddie pushed Avery in the creek.

Normally when that happened, everyone ended up in the water. Eddie usually started it, then several of us would gang up and push him in, and he would take several of us with him. Then everyone would jump in. We'd end the baseball game, and all of us would go swimming. This day it didn't happen.

Eddie hadn't noticed Avery's new shoes when he pushed him in the creek.

All of us kids worked in the fields in the summer and made good money. After most of us were paid, we would save some and then go to buy things for ourselves. We would typically celebrate our windfalls with a stop at the store for a Moon Pie and Coke.

Avery was thirteen and the youngest boy of a large family of sharecroppers. When Avery got paid, he took every penny to his parents, and they used the money for medical expenses, groceries, clothes for the family, the light bill, and to buy fuel for the furnace. Avery didn't get to keep any for himself, not even for a Moon Pie and Coke.

Avery had saved for months so he could buy himself a new pair of shoes. His old shoes were completely worn out, and he was embarrassed to wear them. He had used tape and newspaper to patch them.

And now he had bought a new pair of shoes. A fine pair of leather shoes that would last him a long time if he took care of them, and he sure would because he knew how hard it was to save for them. He was wearing them that day when Eddie pushed him in the creek.

When Avery hit the water, he went stark raving mad. He lost all control and started crying and cursing. Charging up the bank, he went immediately to Eddie and started throwing punches and yelling, "I had my new shoes on. Why didn't you let me take my shoes off before you pushed me in?"

We all figured Eddie would beat him up. He surely didn't want to be embarrassed by Avery who was smaller and weaker. Avery hitting Eddie was like a tadpole smacking a whale. We circled around to see what would happen next.

Eddie, who was already the biggest and strongest in the group, grew a foot taller that day. He recognized the hurt in Avery's heart and saw it in his eyes. He saw the pain that had built up in Avery from a lifetime of poverty. Everyone had more than Avery did.

Avery had worked himself to death to help support his family, and then when he finally saved enough to buy a nice pair of shoes, Eddie had pushed him in the creek.

Eddie didn't swing back. When Avery wore himself out, Eddie grabbed him and hugged him. Both of them were crying.

Bobby took his shirt off and asked Avery to give him his shoes. He then dried them off with his shirt. Brenda went to the house and brought back a shoe brush, a shoeshine rag, and some shoe polish.

Jimmy told Avery that to get a good shine you need to get the leather a little wet. The girls started polishing the shoes.

"I'm sorry," Eddie said. Avery accepted the apology then apologized himself for getting so angry.

We all sat around Avery in the pasture. It must have looked strange for anyone who may have passed by, just a bunch of kids sitting as a group in a cow pasture next to the creek.

One of the guys said, "Avery, we respect you for what you've done for your family. We knew times were hard for you and that you were struggling, but we didn't know what to say."

Then everyone else pitched in with comments. "We're proud of you."

"Yeah, Avery, we care about you."

Our simple little words of encouragement provided a healing salve to Avery's heart. Some of his frustrations of growing up poor fell away, and all of us grew a lot that day. And you know, I think Avery's shoes looked better than they did when they were brand new.

There is nothing better than the encouragement of a good friend.
— KATHARINE BUTLER HATHAWAY

Dear Lord,

Open my eyes to those around me who need to be encouraged. Make me compassionate. Make me a good friend. Remind me that others need to hear the words that are in my heart. Thank you for the encouragement that you've placed in your Word.

Amen.

AGING

CLINGING LIKE A WAISTBAND

SUE MOORE—*speaker and writer*

Casting all your care upon Him, for He cares for you.
—1 PETER 5:7

The ringing phone pulls me from sleep. *Not again, Lord! Is he okay?*

"Hi, Dad." The words are groggy as my sleep-fogged brain attempts to function.

"I'm up and ready to go. Are you up?" he asks me.

I squint at the glowing numbers on the clock. "No, it's only 2:00 in the morning. You can go back to bed, Dad."

Confusion colors his voice. "Only 2:00 in the morning? Somebody's got to quit messing with my clocks around here...."

Lord, help me to reassure and calm him. "It's okay, Dad. No big deal. You can sleep for four more hours." As I encouraged my dad to go back to bed, I knew sleep would elude me in the next hours as I prayed for him and asked God to give me his strength and wisdom as dad's caregiver.

Misreading the clock, restless sleep, and time-of-day confusion are just a few of the many symptoms of Alzheimer's—the terminal disease that is taking over my dad's mind and body as it deteriorates his brain. He experiences hallucinations. Short-term memories disappear. His mind goes to the past to retrieve memories of times and people long ago.

Dad struggles to find words to communicate what he wants to say. His alarm clock recently became "that thing you turn on and off like water." At times, he just gives up trying to find the words he is looking for—the words he searches for desperately in order to speak of what he still sees and pictures clearly in his mind.

As with other Alzheimer's patients, there are times when Dad doesn't recognize his home, so he packs his things and waits for me to pick him up so he can "go home."

As I pray for my dad, I take my questions and pain to the Lord to receive comfort. *How can I help him, Father—how can I better honor him? How can I make each moment that we have together enjoyable, even when he gets to the point of no longer recognizing me as his daughter? How can I calm his fears and frustrations from living in a world that is becoming increasingly confusing and unfamiliar to him? When will he need more care than I can give?*

Help me to take one day at a time, trusting that you will take care of tomorrow. Give me your strength, wisdom, and divine love so I can help Dad through this, dear Lord. Comfort me so I can comfort him....

In this time of parenting my parent, God reminds me of his words in Jeremiah 13, where he says he created his people to cling to him like a waistband. I cling to Jesus for dear life, knowing that he alone is my hope, my strength, and my great peace in the midst of the uncertainty of Dad's disease. Just as my dad clings to me, I cling as intimately as a waistband to the God who loves us passionately and holds the unknown future in his hands.

I remember how Dad pursued Jesus when I was a child. He was firm in his faith, and by his quiet example, I could see how personal God was to him. While Dad held on to Jesus tightly, I held onto Dad's hand—going wherever he led, knowing I was safe and loved, trusting him to take care of me.

Now the table is turned. My dad clings to me, trusting me to take care of *him*. And I follow hard after my heavenly Father, holding to his simple words of comfort, trusting him to love and care for us both and to keep us safe.

I grip tightly, knowing that God will walk us through this valley of the shadow of death where we fear no evil, for he is with us. He comforts us with his intimate presence and unfailing love as we cling to him—and because of that, all is still well.

When you have nothing left but God …
you become aware that God is enough.

—A. Maude Royden

Dear Lord,
Help me to cling to you today for strength and comfort. Let
my life be an example of your loving care. Let my hands be
extensions of your hands as I nurture my loved one. Grant
patience where needed, calm my fears, and help me to
remember that your grace is sufficient for all that I need.
Amen.

THE LETTER OF ENCOURAGEMENT

This is one of the most difficult communications to create. Not because it's tough to write, but because it's often difficult to keep the focus on the "Dear" person you're writing to. In our hurry-scurry world, we may have the best intentions of offering encouragement to a struggling single dad, the mom with four children under four, the friend who lost a spouse—but instead we start telling our own tales, making ourselves the point of the letter. Picture the addressee in your mind and add personal anecdotes only if they're uplifting. Don't tell an expectant mother that she's about to experience the trauma of her life. Let her know that soon she'll be holding her own precious baby. Keep your encouragement encouraging ... and keep the focus off yourself.

JOY

A JOYFUL NOISE

JOY SCARLATTA IERON—*organist and keyboardist*

Oh come, let us sing to the LORD!
Let us shout joyfully to the Rock of our salvation.
—PSALM 95:1

I'm a musician. But I'm not a soloist. I know that. And if you were to hear me, you'd be quick to agree. So, when I received a call from a Christian friend (who knew me as a keyboard player at her women's Bible group) asking me to join a professional traveling singing group, I was about to accept as pianist—when she instead announced that my role would be low alto. The group would consist of four singers—three sopranos, and *me.*

We began rehearsals, and I felt inadequate from the start. Such beautiful voices surrounded me. And then there was my foghorn. Or so it seemed to me. I had no trouble learning my parts, but in those early concerts I found myself keeping my head down as

I sang, sad that I hadn't received an outstanding voice from God. I wondered if I was really an essential part of the blend.

A few months into the experience, Mary, the leader, called in a professional voice coach to help us enhance our sound and to "take us to the next level." And that's when the simple little words came into play for me.

After the coach listened to our rehearsal, she was ready to give us her critique. I can hardly recall how she critiqued the others, but I'll never forget what she said to me, "Joy, your low part sustains the group from below, just as the bass part sustains a four-part choir. Hold your head high and gently sing your part with confidence."

Yes, Joy. Tone back on that foghorn—sing gently. But sing proudly, because God has entrusted you with a gift that may not sparkle like the soprano or call attention to itself like the lead, but it is essential nonetheless.

I took that advice to heart. My solos were few during the nearly eight years we traveled the Midwest and sang in churches of every denomination, and even on international television. But my newfound confidence allowed me to close nearly every concert with an invitation to come to know God personally through his son, Jesus Christ.

The little words that encouraged me to stay with the ministry allowed me the privilege of introducing countless women (and men) to the God we were singing about.

Oh, and when the coach returned a year later for a second consultation, her comment to me was, "See, I knew you had it in you!" And I guess I did, after all.

Use what talents you possess: The woods would be very silent if no birds sang there except those that sang best.

—HENRY VAN DYKE

Dear Lord,
Help me to value the talents you've given me and help
me to use them for your glory. I thank you for blessing
my life in so many ways. Let the joyful song in my heart
spill over into the lives of others.
Amen.

PRAYER

A Prisoner of Love

Kathi Macias—*award-winning author*

*Be anxious for nothing, but in everything by prayer
and supplication, with thanksgiving, let your
requests be made known to God.*
—Philippians 4:6

One of my most prized possessions, as far as books go, is a book titled *Sitting by My Laughing Fire* by the late Ruth Bell Graham. I love the content, but I consider the book extra special because a prisoner at San Quentin gave it to me.

I visited San Quentin as part of a weekend ministry, and a prisoner heard me talk of my struggle with my youngest son who was my prodigal at the time. He wanted to give me something to encourage me, but being in prison, he had little in the way of material things to offer.

He knew about Ruth Graham's book *Prodigals and Those Who Love Them,* but he didn't have a copy. However, he did have

Sitting by My Laughing Fire, which his mother had given him before she died. He had read and reread it countless times, making notes on each occasion.

He insisted I take the book and read it when I became discouraged about my son. "May it remind you that my mom prayed me into the kingdom. And if God can get hold of me, he can save anybody."

Tears misted my eyes as I stood there that day holding his well-worn treasure. I had visited the prison to give inspiration and cheer to the inmates. Instead, I received an unexpected gift as God used one of them to provide the encouraging words I needed to keep praying—and hoping—for my prodigal son.

I remember my mother's prayers, and they have always
followed me. They have clung to me all my life.

—ABRAHAM LINCOLN

Dear Lord,
Thanks for being with me in the darkest places. You
hold me tight even when I try to hide. Please fill me
with hope though sometimes I'm afraid. Keep my
children and grandchildren on the path that leads to
you—and draw them back when they stray.
Amen.

FORGIVENESS

An Unlikely Pair

Diane Jones

But I say to you, love your enemies, bless those who curse you,
do good to those who hate you, and pray for those who
spitefully use you and persecute you.

—Matthew 5:44

In God's Word, he tells me to love my enemies and pray for those who persecute me. But who is my enemy? The grouchy neighbor yelling at my kids? The driver giving me an angry fist on the freeway?

When our nation was attacked on September 11, 2001, I was able to put a face to my enemy. Those few men represented millions who hated us. People who wanted to kill my family and me. I was supposed to pray for them?

Eighteen months later, my husband and I put our nineteen-year-old son on a plane to boot camp. His goal was to move from Marine to FBI officer. At the time of his deferred enlistment, we weren't at war with Iraq.

Things changed quickly. His first deployment after Infantry School would be a combat duty in Fallujah, Iraq. We hit our knees in fervent prayer. As a mom, I thought of the Iraqi mothers sending their sons to war. The pain was immense.

I prayed that a liberated Iraqi people would also find freedom from the tyranny in their hearts. That was the only way they could serve the one true God. But I felt the Lord was asking me to do more.

What? Tell me, Lord.

In the fall of 2006, my husband and I had dinner with Pastor Tom Doyle and his wife, JoAnn. The Doyles minister to believers in the Middle East. JoAnn and E3 Partners would take a women's group from America to participate in the only conference in the world for MBB women. MBB stands for Muslim Background Believers.

If I chose to join the group, we would spend a week in Jordan teaching them to use the EvangeCube, a tool that presents the gospel in visual form, enabling them to share their faith in their own country. We would also teach from the Scriptures on marriage, family, and finances. Practical truths relevant around the globe. More than one hundred women from dozens of different countries, including Iraq, were expected.

God tugged on my heart. *Was this my chance to serve? Yes, Lord!*

I joined the Doyles along with ten American women for this weeklong conference.

During devotions the first day in Amman, a woman named Vivian spoke up. "My husband and my children were killed by an American soldier."

Every word was like a bullet to the soul.

Her husband, two sons, and a daughter were caught in fatal cross fire. She witnessed the shooting and then comforted her children as they died in her arms.

How could I help her? Most likely she would hate me because my son served in the U.S. military. My heart ached for Vivian. She was a frightened mother just like me.

During breaks, we ministered to the whole person by giving hand massages and facials. This closeness allowed us to show tenderness. We talked, cried, and prayed with these believers. I finished one pair of hands and turned to the next.

Vivian sat down.

I introduced myself, and as I gently rubbed her hands, I asked her quiet questions. She told of the loss of her family in Baghdad, her journey to the Lord, and how he allowed her to lead her parents and brother's family to Jesus.

Should I speak? God gave me the courage to tell my story. "My son is a Marine who fought in Fallujah and Ramadi." With heartfelt emotion, I told her of my prayers for families like hers. I hoped they would find the God of love. I was honored to have her as a sister in the Lord, and I asked her forgiveness.

"I have forgiven the American soldiers who killed my family," she said. It touched her to know that so many were praying for her country. "Thank you for your prayers," she said.

God used those words of forgiveness, and he healed us in those moments. We prayed, hugged, and wept together. We were sisters in the faith who could have been enemies if not for the blood of Jesus Christ and the power of prayer.

Without forgiveness life is governed by …
an endless cycle of resentment and retaliation.

—ROBERTO ASSAGIOLI

Dear Lord,
Give me a forgiving heart. Help me to love those who've wronged me. Help me to reach out to those who need to feel your kindness and love. Thank you for your forgiveness on the many occasions when I've failed you.
Amen.

THE E-MAIL OF ENCOURAGEMENT

E-mail messages rule our lives. We get them all the time from multiple sources. Sometimes the contents make us cringe. Like our snail mail, the incoming electronic correspondence often falls in the "junk" and "very junk" categories. That's why it's always a pleasure to get an honest you-to-me message. Not a forward, but a note that expresses a genuine word or two of encouragement. Send your spouse a simple "I love you," "I miss you," or "Can hardly wait to see you." Let your loved ones know you're thinking about them ... and then get back to work!

COMPASSION

You Look Like a Princess

Michelle Cox

Love one another as I have loved you.
—John 15:12

The stylishly dressed young woman approached the older couple sitting at a table in the restaurant. "You don't know who I am, do you?"

Jacquie Sexton smiled sweetly. In her role as pastor's wife, she had met thousands of people. "Honey, I can't imagine not remembering such a beautiful young woman, but I'm sorry, I can't place you. Please, sit down and join us."

"I didn't expect you to recognize me. I look far different than I did when you knew me." Tears misted her eyes. "Do you remember taking a dirty, unkempt little girl home with you one Sunday many years ago? I'm that girl. You would have known me as Mandy."

The memory clicked into place in Mrs. Sexton's mind in

vivid detail. She had noticed the child and her mother the first Sunday they visited the little white church where her husband was pastor. Years of hopelessness and hard times had etched themselves into the mother's features. Mandy's little face was unwashed, her clothing dirty, and her hair tangled and limp.

Mrs. Sexton welcomed them with her trademark warmth. Then she said, "My daughter is a few years older than your little girl. They could play together if you'll let her go home with us this afternoon. I'll bring her back to church tonight."

The Sextons treated Mandy like an honored guest, seating her at their dining-room table, filling her plate with delicious, home-cooked food.

After the girls had played, Mrs. Sexton said, "Honey, would you like to take a bubble bath?" Making it fun, she plopped some bubbles on Mandy's nose then washed the dirt from her face. She lathered her hair with sweet-smelling shampoo and kindness, combing gently through the tangles.

Then she dried and curled Mandy's hair. "While you girls were playing, I hemmed one of my daughter's slips, and I found one of her dresses that might be the right size. Would you like to try it on? If the dress fits, you can wear it to church tonight and then you can keep it."

With a little alteration, the dress fit perfectly. "Mandy, would you like to see what you look like? There's a mirror over there. Honey, you look like a princess!"

Mandy looked at the image in the mirror. The child who looked back at her was one she'd never seen before. "Is that really me? I *do* look like a princess."

That night when the Sextons took Mandy back to church, her own mother didn't recognize her.

They lost touch with the mother and daughter not long after that, but Mrs. Sexton had often wondered what had happened to Mandy.

She looked across the table at the polished, perfectly groomed young woman. "You've turned out beautiful, honey. And it looks like things are going well for you."

"That's why I wanted to speak to you today. I wanted to say thank you. I'm where I am today because of your kindness." She swiped at the moisture on her cheeks. "Through all the dreary days of my childhood, I never forgot how I felt that day when you told me I looked like a princess. I determined that things would be different when I was grown. And no matter how tough things were at home, I always remembered there was a princess hidden inside me."

Even if you can't prevent another's sorrow, caring will lessen it.

— FRANK A. CLARK

Dear Lord,
Open my eyes to those around me who need to feel
your compassion. Let my life be a vessel so filled with
your love that it overflows into the lives of others.
Give me words of kindness and understanding that
will be a blessing to those who need them.
Amen.

PARENTING

A Valuable Lesson

Ron DiCianni—*commercial illustrator*

A wise son heeds his father's instruction.
—Proverbs 13:1

Parenting should come with a handbook. No, not one that tells what to do when a baby cries or how to change a diaper. There are plenty of those around. I needed one that told me how to be smarter than my kids, even in the early years.

One day in particular that I could have used that book was when my wife, our two little boys, ages seven and four, and I drove to Wisconsin to buy some harmless fireworks for the upcoming Fourth of July holiday.

Not far into the trip, the kids began to ask where we were going to eat. As we began to ponder options, our oldest said he had a taste for Mexican food. Well, kinda like what happens when we fed our dog table scraps, certain foods had a tendency to give back more than expected at very unwanted times.

We tried to use the old distraction method by bringing up other, milder choices, or even pointing out other places that we saw as we were driving by, but all to no avail. He had made up his mind that Mexican food was what he wanted, and that was final.

My next step was to try reasoning with the child. I calmly explained that he might regret that choice later in the day. I reminded him that we were taking a long ride and that we wouldn't be home for a while.

I might as well have tried talking to the headrest. The more I reasoned, the greater he expressed the intensity of his choice. He assured us that all would be well, in spite of our worries. After all, he *was* seven and surely knew what was best! I continued to warn of the consequences, knowing that it was better for him not to have the spicy Mexican food.

Pulling in to the closest Mexican restaurant (yeah, we caved), he knew exactly what he wanted, which we promptly ordered. We ate, he smiled, and on we went with the trip. Well, at least for about forty minutes or so. That's when he doubled over in stomach pain.

We had to cancel the trip and turn around to go home when he finally admitted that the food did him in. I exploded with a barrage of the "I told you so's" to which he responded with some words that forever changed my parenting skills.

He looked up and said, "You're the parent. Why didn't you just say no?"

That was a pivotal day in my life as I learned that saying no is a valid answer to my children in some situations. However, as I thought about the situation, I realized that wasn't all my son's words had taught me—he'd taught me a valuable lesson that day.

I wonder how many times God has to say no when he has *my* best interests in mind? I know I've often been just like my son, sure that I knew the perfect solution for what would be best for my life.

And I'm sure that when God said no, I threw tantrums and accused him of a lot of unkind things that showed my immaturity.

God has had to remind me that *he* is the Father and that he has the right and the responsibility to give the answers he knows I need, and to deny what he knows will be my undoing.

Looking back, I'm glad that God said no to some things I begged for, even when I thought he was being cruel and strict. That's what a good dad does!

Some people think that parents teach their children, but not in this instance. My son's wise words that day reminded me to yield graciously to the all-knowing wisdom of my heavenly Father whenever he says no to me.

The parent's life is the child's copybook.

—ANONYMOUS

Dear Lord,

I'm grateful that you know what's best for me. Give me a heart that will listen to your instruction. Help me to yield graciously to your wisdom knowing that you love me and you have a plan for my life. Thank you for being my heavenly Father. I desire to be like you.

Amen.

RELATIONSHIPS

QUEEN FOR A LIFETIME

CARLY W. DIXON

And now abide faith, hope, love, these three;
but the greatest of these is love.
—1 CORINTHIANS 13:13

My husband had always been good to me, but several months ago his words affected my life in an unexpected way. In the midst of a conversation we were having, he told me, "All I want is for you to always feel like a queen."

My heart was touched as I heard him verbalize those simple words. You see, they were in stark contrast to words I endured in a five-year relationship in college.

In that destructive relationship, my boyfriend often made me feel unworthy. On many occasions, I remember him telling me that I was lucky to have him because no one else would want me.

I don't know why I believed his cruel remarks. I wasn't particularly unattractive or unpleasant. I had many friends and most people seemed to like me. In my tender heart, the words my ex-boyfriend hurled at me day after day far outweighed the evidence.

My personality changed as I began to believe the things he said. During that terrible relationship, the light in my soul flickered out like a pilot light on a cold December morning. I left that relationship broken, with little or no self-esteem and very little trust in anyone. My traumatized emotions left me dysfunctional in every way.

Then I met my husband and the once-extinguished light in my soul began to flicker again.

Now I had these new precious words from my husband to add to my treasure chest of cherished memories. And they reminded me of how much healing has occurred in my heart and life over the past eight years.

I consciously realized that, to him I was precious and cherished. Those simple words enabled me to see that my heavenly Father cherishes me as well. What an amazing feeling!

And what a reminder that encouragement in marriage can be such a powerful tool. Those words can build self-esteem or destroy it.

As in my case, such a simple sentence changed my life. Those words changed the way I viewed myself, and the way I viewed my husband and my heavenly Father.

His comment made me feel like the girl on the bench at a high school dance who has just been asked to dance by the most popular boy in school.

Once I felt unworthy; now I feel cherished and loved. Since that time, my husband and I have started a new habit. We have a note on our fridge reminding us to encourage one another.

Most of the time, the comments aren't mushy, but more along the lines of "You did an awesome job washing the car" or "I really like your new haircut."

Encouragement in a marriage can make a husband feel like a man, and a woman feel like a princess … or a queen. I know from experience. Those simple little words my husband said that day have changed my life forever.

Anybody can be a heart specialist.
The only requirement is loving somebody.
—ANGIE PAPADAKIS

Dear Lord,
Guard my relationships. Help my words never to
wound those I love. Instead, make me an encourager.
Help my words to share blessings, love, and
compassion to those you've placed in my life.
Amen.

TIME

GLENN FORD'S TIMELY ADVICE

KEN WALES—*Hollywood producer*

To everything there is a season,
a time for every purpose under heaven.
—ECCLESIASTES 3:1

Enticed by the story of Lana Turner's discovery in a drugstore, thousands of young people flock every year to Hollywood—the film capital of the world—to seek their fame and fortune. Because I grew up in California among actors and filmmakers, I knew Lana Turner's *real* story.

Sorry to disappoint you, but the drugstore tale was only a myth. People are seldom "discovered" in Hollywood. Many people try to make it in the business, but few do. To survive in the highly competitive movie industry takes faith, hard work, and perseverance. In spite of all this knowledge, I still dreamed of Hollywood.

I was a PK (preacher's kid), and because of the many evils in Hollywood, family and friends often tried to dissuade me from my career choice. They urged me to follow my dad into the ministry, but I already knew what I wanted to do with my life—I wanted to produce family films. I knew that God's timing was always perfect, so I would prepare myself and then wait for an opportunity.

"My ministry is in film, not in the pulpit." I explained, respectfully. I'm not so sure they believed it possible.

Finally, at age fourteen, I got my first big break in the movie industry. I was hired to run the projector at the legendary Aero Theater on Montana Avenue in Santa Monica—shades of the movie, *Cinema Paridiso*. (Everybody has to start somewhere don't they?) As the film reels rolled, I studied the scenes and dreamed of the day when I could create my own movies.

Living in California had other advantages too—especially its beaches. I became a surfer. As a teenager, I surfed on Malibu Beach with the *real* Gidget—the one who became famous in the movie by the same name. Her screenwriter father wrote about his daughter's surfing adventures. I was an extra in that movie, and my surfing prowess eventually led to a small part as a surfer in the movie *Where the Boys Are*.

Although as a teenager I wasn't passionate about acting, I immediately saw it as an opportunity to learn the film business. Soon I began auditioning for parts in movies and television. After several small roles in films, I received the Glenn Ford Award during my senior year at Santa Monica High School.

At the time I received the award, Glenn Ford was considered one of the greatest actors in Hollywood, and he was certainly among the most famous. He had skyrocketed to fame in his role opposite starlet Rita Hayworth in the film *Gilda*. His blockbuster films included *Blackboard Jungle*, *3:10 to Yuma*, and *Teahouse of the August Moon*.

As the award recipient, I had the opportunity to meet Glenn Ford, and he graciously offered to mentor me. I was cast in small parts in several of his films.

Glenn was a consummate professional. He taught me the most important ingredients for success in business—always be well prepared, work hard, and arrive on the set early. But his words that stayed with me throughout my career were, "If you're early, *you're on time*. If you're on time, *you're late*. If you're late, *you're fired*."

While at USC Film School, I played Glenn's FBI sidekick in the film *Experiment in Terror*. That set is where I met the famous director Blake Edwards, who later gave me my chance to produce films in Hollywood.

Throughout the years, I have fulfilled my dreams of producing family films such as *Revenge of the Pink Panther*, the CBS series *Christy*, and the feature film *Amazing Grace*. And I never forgot Glenn's wise advice.

When Glenn Ford died at age ninety, I was invited to speak at his grave site. Arriving extra early in his honor, I sat alone in the chapel with the body of my friend and mentor. As I reflected on his life and career, I thought of what he had meant to me personally and as a filmmaker.

I could still hear him utter the words that have served me best in my career and in my life, "If you are early, *you're on time*. If you're on time, *you're late*. If you're late, *you're fired*."

Although I knew his spirit was no longer there, I spoke to his remains, "I'm early so I'm guess I'm on time, dear friend."

But I knew Glenn Ford couldn't hear those words. I knew he had already arrived in heaven—not too early, not too late, but right on time. God's timing!

How you spend your time is more important
than how you spend your money. Money mistakes can be
corrected, but time is gone forever.

—DAVID B. NORRIS

Dear Lord,
Thank you for always being on time whenever I need
you. Help me to use my time in a manner that will
make you proud of me. Remind me that each moment of
my life is a gift from you.
Amen.

HEALING

AN UNEXPECTED RESPONSE

JERILYN S. ROBINSON

I shall not die, but live, and declare the works of the LORD.
—PSALM 118:17

I'll never forget the moment the doctor said, "You have twenty to twenty-four months to live." Those words—with the prognosis of inoperable pancreatic cancer—changed our lives forever. My husband, Don, and I held on to the loving, comforting words of Psalm 91:

> He who dwells in the secret place of the Most High
>> Shall abide under the shadow of the Almighty.
> I will say of the LORD, "*He is* my refuge and my fortress;
>> My God, in Him I will trust."
>
> Because you have made the LORD, *who* is my refuge,
>> *Even* the Most High, your dwelling place,
> No evil shall befall you,

Nor shall any plague come near your dwelling;
For He shall give His angels charge over you,
To keep you in all your ways.

"Because he has set his love upon Me, therefore I will deliver him;
I will set him on high, because he has known My name.
He shall call upon Me, and I will answer him;
I *will be* with him in trouble;
I will deliver him and honor him.
With long life I will satisfy him,
And show him My salvation."

I had first noticed there was a problem on the afternoon of Christmas Day, 2005. It was Sunday morning and off to church we went to celebrate the birth of Jesus. The morning was glorious. That afternoon, however, things started to change. I couldn't explain it—I just didn't feel right.

On Monday morning, my bodily function showed that something wasn't normal. Everything was the wrong color, and my skin started to turn yellow. By Wednesday, it was apparent that something was definitely wrong. We called our family physician and were able to see him on Friday, December 30.

He ordered an ultrasound exam, which showed a blockage near my pancreas. Then he immediately ordered a CT scan. The results were still inconclusive.

The doctor referred us to the gastrointestinal department at the Cleveland Clinic in Ohio. They did an endoscopic ultrasound on January 3. The results were "most likely cancer," but surgery would be required for further diagnosis. Surgery was scheduled for January 9.

The surgeon gave us the grim results. The tumor had encapsulated my common bile duct, and the feelers had penetrated the arteries of the liver, rendering the tumor inoperable. Without treatment, I had ten to twelve months to live; with treatment, I could double that life expectancy.

I underwent six weeks of radiation therapy and weekly chemotherapy that would continue indefinitely.

My husband and I spent many hours on our knees praying to God for his healing power. Things seemed so hopeless but those words, "I will be with you" brought me comfort. We were both overwhelmed with sadness, resigned to the inevitable. We couldn't sleep or eat.

With hope and joy gone, my husband turned to the Lord in prayer for comfort. On his knees in the upstairs bedroom, he asked the Lord to take this unbearable burden from him. Don reported that at that moment of surrender he felt the suffocating weight of despair lifted from his shoulders and an amazing sense of peace and serenity. This was the first of many mercies the Lord would provide during our trial.

We spent many long days in the car driving between West Virginia and the Cleveland Clinic for treatment. I underwent CT scans every three months following radiation and chemotherapy.

The first CT scan in May 2006 showed a decrease in the size of the tumor—enough to encourage the oncologist to contact the surgeon about whether surgery to remove the tumor was now an option. The surgeon remained confident that I was nonresectable and told us to live out the rest of my life doing what I wanted and needed to do.

The next two CT scans (in July and November 2006) showed no definite change—the tumor was neither shrinking nor spreading.

In March 2007, however, something was different. The CT scan showed that the lymph nodes had increased in size by approximately 25 percent. The oncologist reported that the chemotherapy drug I was on was no longer working.

We received this report on April 25, 2007, just a couple of weeks before our planned move from West Virginia to Arizona. The doctor suggested taking the time off and giving my body a rest from the chemotherapy. Then we could discuss a new course of treatment with our Arizona oncologist.

We arrived in Arizona on May 5 and met with our local oncologist on May 10. He suggested a much more aggressive chemotherapy treatment to begin immediately. I said no. After having had no chemo since April 11, I was feeling pretty good; I felt strong and healthy and thought perhaps it was time for "man to move over and let God work."

The oncologist ordered another CT scan on May 25, 2007.

At 8:30 in the evening on May 30, the oncologist called us at home and stated that he had the results of the CT scan. What he said next stunned and electrified us, "The scan shows *no* cancer, *no* tumor, and the lymph nodes are *normal* in size."

My husband and I fell on our knees and thanked God for the miraculous healing he did in my body. There was no medical explanation. Pancreatic cancer doesn't just go away. Remission is not common. How did this happen? Only one explanation—it was the power of prayer and the grace of God.

God heard our cries and responded as only he can—with loving tenderness, grace, and mercy. And he proved to me that his words, "I will be with you" in Psalm 91 were true. I called upon him, and he answered me. He was with me and he delivered me.

If God gave His own Son for us, how could He ever bring
Himself to desert us in small things?

— MARTIN LUTHER

Dear Lord,
Thank you for your presence during the dark times in my
life. Thank you for being a God who answers prayer and
for your heart of compassion that hurts when I hurt. I'm
grateful that nothing is too hard for you.
Amen.

THE CARD OF ENCOURAGEMENT

It's so easy! Make your own or let the greeting-card company do the talking. Usually you can find a card that says exactly what you would have said if words came easy. Make a habit of picking up a card now and then. If married, start with a special message for your spouse. Sign the card and hide it under his or her pillow. Or on the front seat of the car. Or on top of the washing machine. Mail a card to your parents, coworkers, friends, pastor, teacher, or doctor. Bet your dentist doesn't get a "thank-you" too often! Add him or her to your list, and you'll be sure to brighten a day with your simple act of encouragement.

COMFORT

Wisdom from a Child

Aaron Swavely—*devotional writer*

For God so loved the world that He gave His only
begotten Son, that whoever believes in Him should
not perish but have everlasting life.

—John 3:16

Winter, 2000. I headed home after trying to encourage a friend who lost both mother and sister within a month. The man was beyond consolation. And he was stumped, wondering why God would take such wonderful people. Women who had never harmed anyone.

The "why" question was always the toughest to answer.

"Simply trust the Lord" was no cliché, but the truth I wanted him to hear. He wasn't listening.

Fortunately, God sent a sweet angel to help me share that message. My daughter, Alisha, almost seven, folded a sympathy card for him from construction paper and decorated her masterpiece with Magic Markers. She loved making things.

Earlier that year, she had made bookmarks for her entire Sunday-school class. With her trusty Magic Markers, she used scrap paper to say "Jesus loves you" and "God loves you." Her bookmarks weren't complete until she added special hand-colored hearts.

Alisha had proudly brought me one.

Mine said "Jesus loves you," and my heart was colored orange.

On Easter Eve, Alisha celebrated her seventh birthday.

Six days later, our family was in a devastating car accident, and my faith was rocked as I faced the crisis of my life. My wife, Amy, and my son, Jordan, were badly injured. Little Alisha lapsed into a coma. After five days praying for a miracle, Alisha met Jesus face-to-face.

The most difficult thing to comprehend was why God would take my daughter. *Why?* Did God hate me? Had I done something to deserve this? Suddenly, I connected with the confusion my friend had felt.

Closing my eyes, I could almost hear my daughter's sweet voice saying her favorite phrase, "Daddy, Jesus loves you."

Sometimes we take those words so lightly that the significance fades. And to be honest, I'm not sure I got the meaning myself until that moment when I held my dying daughter's hand.

"Jesus loves you." They were simple words from a child with wisdom beyond her years. Alisha understood. Telling others that Jesus loves them can change their lives.

God proved His love on the cross. When Christ hung, and bled, and died, it was God saying to the world, "I love you."

—BILLY GRAHAM

Dear Lord,

Thank you for loving me. I'm overwhelmed that the God of the universe knows my name and that you gave your son to die for me. Thank you for the gift of your salvation, for your love letter—the Bible—that brings me comfort and strength, and for your daily presence in my life. Help me to share your message of hope "Jesus loves you" with those who need to hear.

Amen.

FRIENDSHIP

YOU ARE A GREAT MOTHER

MARY GILZEAN

A friend loves at all times.
—PROVERBS 17:17

December, 1987. My father had died, and my mailbox overflowed with condolence cards. Among them was an envelope adorned with a red heart address label on the upper-left corner. The colorful sticker caught my attention. So did the message in Mary's handwritten letter.

She spoke of her sorrow at Dad's passing. Then she said something I desperately needed to hear. "Sweetie, I know how hard it is to be home with little ones. You are balancing a baby on one hip, carrying a laundry basket on the other, all the while chasing after a toddler."

She was right. As a young mother, I was completely and utterly overwhelmed. My son, Christopher, was nine months old, and my daughter, Jaqualine, was smack-dab in the middle of the terrific two's. With my dad's passing, I felt more drained than usual.

My own mother, unfortunately, provided no comfort. Mom never showed affection. Words like "I love you" evaded her vocabulary.

Mary's letter was like water poured on dry, cracked soil. As I read her words of encouragement, tears streamed down my face. *Finally, someone understands what I'm going through.* Mary got it: Parenting was hard.

None of my girlfriends had children yet, so I couldn't share my frustrations. All my neighbors worked outside the home, so the streets were deserted when I took my two for walks. I felt alone and unsure of myself as a mom.

Conflicting emotions swirled. I wanted to be a good mother—to nurture my children, play with them, read to them, and kiss their skinned knees. But as I felt my careful plans for the day slip away, I was overwhelmed by the kids' clinginess. Drained and testy, I doubted my parenting skills.

After reading Mary's letter, I immediately responded. I thanked her for her kind words and asked for some parenting advice. That first exchange set off a pen-pal relationship that lasted for years.

Mary and I were a perfect match because we both loved to write. And we both helped each other. For me, Mary—or Ma Nil—became a mentor, friend, and surrogate mother. For her, I was a daughter in need of advice.

Ma Nil's two daughters were in college pursuing advanced degrees. Mary was proud of them but wanted to feel needed. And I needed someone. In her envelopes, I found diaper coupons, silly cartoons, and remembrances of what her babies did so many years ago. Every week I reaped a wealth of child-rearing wisdom.

The words that meant the most to me were "My dear, you are a great mother."

How wonderful to hear such encouragement. My preschoolers were throwing tantrums and my feet were stuck in spilled Kool-Aid. I wondered if I'd make it. Mary's letters gave me hope.

Nearly twenty years later I still cherish those letters. I have a treasure box filled with them. Sometimes I reread one. I think about how Ma Nil's words uplifted me during that challenging, tiring time. She encouraged me to keep going.

Each envelope has a bright red heart sticker on the corner, and all are stuffed full of the most precious words I have ever read.

Friendship is one of the sweetest joys of life.
Many might have failed beneath the bitterness
of their trial had they not found a friend.

—CHARLES H. SPURGEON

Dear Lord,
Help me to be a friend to those who need one.
Help me to rejoice in their good times and to
be steadfast during difficult days. Thank you
for being my dearest friend and for always
being there when I've needed you.
Amen.

CHILDREN

READING LOVE
BETWEEN THE LINES

MICHELLE COX

Behold, children are a heritage from the LORD.
—PSALM 127:3

Among my treasured keepsakes are love letters my husband wrote while we were dating. They are precious to me, but I must admit that one of my sweetest love letters came from another man. Okay, before you start gasping in disapproval, I'd better explain that the letter writer was a pint-sized replica of my husband. Here's how it happened.

Remembering how much I loved receiving mail when I was a child, I began writing letters to my sons when they were very young. As I slipped into three-year-old Jason's bedroom one night, I heard a sleepy little voice say, "Whatcha doin', Mama?"

Sitting down beside him on the bed, I replied, "I wrote you a letter, and I put it on your dresser so you would find it in the morning. Do you want me to read it to you now?"

He snuggled close and I read,

> *"Dear Jason, Daddy and I love you very much. You are such a good boy and we are thankful that God sent you to our family. Love, Mama."*

After another of those special little-boy hugs, I tucked him back into bed and went downstairs to fold laundry.

Walking upstairs a little later with the clean clothes, I noticed a light in my husband's office. As I reached to turn the light off, I noticed the tiny figure perched on the desk chair. I stepped into the shadows of the room so I could see what he was doing without his seeing me. I watched as he folded a piece of paper and inserted it into an envelope. Then he propped it on my dresser and scampered off to bed.

Opening the envelope, I looked at the page, every line filled with that scrawling imitation of cursive writing used by children who have not yet learned to write. With tear-filled eyes, I thanked God for the special privilege of being a mom. And you know what? "Reading" my letter was easy—I simply read the love written between every line.

And I was reminded once again that those simple little

words of love that we give away are sometimes returned to us as priceless gifts.

Anyone who has known the love of a
child has been blessed indeed.

—MICHELLE COX

Dear Lord,
Thank you for loaning this precious child to me.
Help my hands to be extensions of yours as I teach
this little life about character and love, and about
you. Give me patience and wisdom as I go about
my daily tasks as a parent, and as my child follows
in my footsteps, let them always lead toward you.
Amen.

TOP 10 LIST OF PEOPLE YOU NEED TO SAY "I LOVE YOU" TO

Spouse

Children

Parents

Siblings

Grandparents

Friends

Enemies

Teachers

Neighbors

Self

SIBLINGS

You're the World's Best Brother

Michelle Cox

Be kindly affectionate to one another with brotherly love, in honor giving preference to one another.

—Romans 12:10

Fifteen-year-old Vicky and eleven-year-old Michael Haynes were like most sisters and brothers. They drove each other nuts. Both knew exactly which buttons to push to irritate the other.

Vicky remembers, "We fought like cats and dogs—especially when our parents were gone. Michael was always getting into my stuff and invading my room. You know, just being a typical little brother."

The two usually went their own way, but one sunny day, they decided to walk together to the K-Mart near their home.

They started down the dirt road, Michael stirring up clouds of dust as he kicked at rocks along the way.

He was chattering away, and for once, Vicky really listened to him. She looked at his freckled face, the straight hair falling across his forehead, his eyes sparkling as he laughed. And it hit her. He really *was* a wonderful little brother. The way he expressed himself, his sense of humor, and his outgoing personality all held the promise of the remarkable young man he was becoming.

She stopped him. "Michael, I need to tell you something. You're the best brother in the world, and I'm really blessed to have you as *my* little brother. I just wanted you to know that."

She hugged him and then the two continued on their way, the words forgotten as they browsed through the displays at the store.

Two days later, Michael died in an accident.

And Vicky remembered those words she had said to her brother, grateful she had taken the opportunity to tell him that he was special to her—while there was still time.

Years later, she realized that on the country road that day, God had visited an insecure teenager who was about to face a loss that would shake her to the core, and he had prepared a way to carry her through—without regrets or guilt.

No, she hadn't realized her and Michael's days would be so short, those moments so fleeting, but for the last forty-five years, the fact that she said those words to her little brother has been a comfort to Vicky's heart.

Why are we so stingy with our words when they have the power
to touch a heart, to change a life, or to brighten someone's day?

—MICHELLE COX

Dear Lord,
Help my words to bless the lives of others. Remind
me to say "I'm proud of you" to those who need to
hear it, "I'm sorry" to those I've wronged, and "I
love you" to those around me. I love you, Lord, and
I thank you for your words that have touched my
life, given me hope, and brought me comfort.
Amen.

What simple little words do you need to say to someone who needs to hear them?

CONTRIBUTORS

Suzanne Alexander lives with her husband and teenage sons, splitting time between Maui and Wisconsin. She is on sabbatical from her work as a physician and is writing her first novel.

Jane Ardelean is a grandmother and retired teacher. She spent most of her teaching years in Dayton, Tennessee, and the American School in Brasilia, Brazil.

Sandi Banks's book, *Anchors of Hope: Finding Peace Amidst the Storms of Life*, offers hope to a hurting world. Other published contributions include stories in *Reader's Digest*, the Cup of Comfort series, and the Kisses of Sunshine series. Sandi has lived, traveled, and ministered in a variety of cultures on six continents and has worked with Summit Ministries since 1989, currently directing Adult Worldview conferences. Visit Sandi at her Web site, www.anchorsofhope.com.

Tatyana Buksh lives with her family in Asheville, North Carolina. Originally from Russia, she is a naturalized U.S. citizen and is a member of Trinity Baptist Church.

Sharon E. Carrns uses every life experience to bring God glory as a wife, mother, author, and part-time small groups director at her church in west Michigan. She has written and taught training programs for ministries and corporations in several states.

S. Truett Cathy is the founder and CEO of Chick-fil-A. Mr. Cathy is largely driven by personal satisfaction and a sense of obligation to the community and its young people. His WinShape Centre® Foundation, founded in 1984, grew from his desire to "shape winners" by helping young people succeed in life through scholarships and other youth-support programs. Visit his Web sites at: www.winshape.org and www.chick-fil-a.com.

Virginia Chatman is a retired elementary school teacher. She taught for thirty years in Dayton, Tennessee. She is a graduate of Miami Bible College and Bryan College.

Jim Daly has been with Focus on the Family since 1989, starting as an assistant to the chairman, and then as vice president of three divisions: International, where he represented Focus in seventy countries; Marketing; and Public Affairs. He became a group vice president in 2003 and CEO in 2004. In March 2005, Jim became the successor to Dr. James Dobson as president and CEO. Jim is married to his wife, Jean, and they have two young sons. He is also the author of *Finding Home*.

Mary E. DeMuth loves to write truth from the inside out. Her books include *Ordinary Mom, Extraordinary God; Building the Christian Family You Never Had; Watching the Tree Limbs; Wishing on Dandelions;* and *Authentic Parenting in a Postmodern Culture.* Mary lives in Texas with her husband, Patrick, and their three children. They recently returned from Southern France where they planted a church.

Ron DiCianni attended the American Academy of Art in Chicago, and then embarked on a career in commercial illustration. Quickly recognized as one of the nation's most talented illustrators, Ron's client list was soon dominated by the top companies in America. In 1989, he produced the painting that started a revolution … *Spiritual Warfare.* What began with one painting led into a whole market for Christian art products, ranging from lithographs to books with a wide variety of derivative products. For more information about Ron visit www.TapestryProductions.com.

Carly W. Dixon lives in North Carolina with her husband, Michael, and her two children, Blake and Natalie. Though a speech pathologist by education, she devotes her days to being a mom and to her ministry of helping women recognize God's faithfulness in their lives and learning to serve him faithfully. For more information on Carly's ministry, visit www.faithfulministries.com.

Sherrie Eldridge is a speaker and author who is passionate about nurturing those touched by adoption. She is the author of the highly acclaimed books *Twenty Things Adopted Kids Wish Their Adoptive Parents Knew, Twenty Life-Transforming Choices Adoptees Need to Make*, and *Forever Fingerprints … An Amazing Discovery for Adopted Children*. She is president of Jewel Among Jewels Adoption Network. Visit her Web site at www.sherrieeldridge.com.

Dr. Edna Ellison is a humorist known as "America's Christian mentoring guru." She's given keynote speeches in London, Frankfurt, Panama City, and many states in the United States, including Hawaii and Alaska. To book her for a speaker or for top-quality mentor training in your civic organization or church, visit her Web site at www.ednaellison.com.

Barb Faust has one delightful daughter and a wonderful son-in-law. Though she considers Colorado her home, she now lives in California to be closer to her granddaughter.

Pat Gelsinger, senior vice president of Intel Corporation, is well known in the technology industry and is currently running the largest business group for the company. He is also an active Christian spokesman in the area of work-life balance, having written *Balancing Your Family, Faith, and Work*. He is married with four children and is active in his church and numerous ministries.

Vicky Haynes Gerald lives in Asheville, North Carolina, where she works as a contract coordinator for an environmental lab company.

Mary Gilzean lives in Sacramento, California. She enjoys writing, scrapbooking, and spending time with her husband and four children. Recently, she learned to sail on the San Francisco Bay, and now looks forward to writing about her adventures at sea.

Sandra Glahn, ThM, teaches at Dallas Theological Seminary, where she is editor-in-chief of *Kindred Spirit* magazine. The author of the Coffee Cup Bible Study series, Glahn has also written a number of medical thrillers, including *Informed Consent*.

Brandon Heath has been a respected songwriter in the Nashville music community for years, collaborating with well-known artists like Bebo Norman, Matt Wertz, and Dave Barnes, to name a few. Heath's debut album *Don't Get Comfortable* has already yielded two hit songs with "I'm Not Who I Was" and "Our God Reigns," which garnered a Dove nomination for worship song of the year. Visit his Web sites at www.brandonheath.net and www.reunionrecords.com.

Dr. Dennis E. Hensley is a professor of English at Taylor University Fort Wayne, where he directs the professional writing major. He is the author of more than fifty books, including *Man to Man: Becoming the Believer God Called You to Be.*

Carlton Hughes is a Professor of Communication at Southeast Kentucky Community and Technical College in Cumberland, Kentucky, and serves as Children's Pastor of Lynch Church of God. He has written VBS curriculum, numerous plays and skits, and has been published in both Christian and secular publications. He and his wife, Katherine, have two sons, Noah and Ethan.

Joy Scarlatta Ieron has been a church organist and keyboardist since age nine. A pastor's daughter, she has worked as an executive assistant, employment recruiter, piano teacher, and most recently as publicist/booking agent for her daughter Julie-Allyson Ieron's conference ministry.

Diane Jones is a mother of four and grandmother of one who lives in Colorado with her husband of thirty-one years. She is a retired nurse and now works as an editor for a publishing firm. She is excited about more opportunities to share her faith wherever God places her.

Karen Kingsbury is America's number one inspirational author, with thirty-four Life-Changing Fiction™ titles and more than six million copies of her books in print. Her novel *Ever After* won the

Evangelical Christian Publishers Association 2007 Book of the Year award—the first time the prize has ever gone to a novel. Karen lives in the Pacific Northwest with her husband, Don, and their six children—three of whom are adopted from Haiti. Visit her Web site at www.karenkingsbury.com.

Ann Kroeker is the author of *The Contemplative Mom* and has contributed to such projects as Lee Strobel and Garry Poole's Experiencing the Passion of Jesus, Faith Under Fire DVD series, and Poole's Tough Questions series, and *Seeker Small Groups.* As an author, wife, and mother of four, Ann appreciates the power of words, still seeking to build people up whenever possible. She no longer sprints, but often runs (slowly) for fitness.

Kathi Macias is an award-winning author of seventeen books, including the best-selling devotional *A Moment a Day.* Books eighteen to twenty are scheduled for 2008–2009 release from New Hope Publishers. Kathi, a popular speaker and Bible teacher, lives in Homeland, California, with her husband, Al. Visit her Web site at www.kathimacias.com.

Sue Moore is a teacher and speaker who writes Bible studies and articles on living out faith in daily life. She lives in Iowa with her husband. They have two adult children. For more information, visit her Web site at www.suemooreonline.com.

Pat Neville works as a real estate/title agent/abstractor in Beaver, Oklahoma. He and his wife, Michelle, have five daughters and two sons. He laughingly refers to himself as a "jack of all trades, master of none."

Leon Overbay shares stories about growing up in the '50s and '60s in the Boones Creek community of rural east Tennessee. He's the vice president of Finance for a Christian distribution company (STL Distributors) by day and a storyteller when the opportunity arises. He is also a founding member of the Jonesborough Storytellers Guild.

Diane Reilly has been happily married to her urologist husband, Bob, for over forty years. They have four married children and sixteen grandchildren. Involved in a number of ministries, they take time out of busy schedules to do short-term mission work in Kenya.

Jerilyn S. Robinson enlisted in the United States Air Force in 1969 and retired as a paralegal after twenty years. She and her husband live in Green Valley, Arizona.

Susie Shellenberger is the editor of *BRIO* magazine and has written forty-five books. She is also the cofounder of Closer: Moms & Daughters—a one-day event for moms and their teen daughters. For more information, go to www.closermomsanddaughters.com.

Lisa Smith is a young lady with Down syndrome who has taken the gift of signing and added to it her unashamed love for the Lord, using her talent to touch the hearts of thousands. She has joined Sandi Patty (and numerous other Christian song artists) at concerts on the Trinity Broadcasting Network, at the Bill Gaither Homecoming, at Women of Faith conferences, and on the *Dr. Phil* show.

Vicki Smith resides in Texas with her husband. They have three children and three beautiful grandchildren. Vicki has been working in city government for twenty years, serving the last sixteen years as the court administrator for the city of Plano. They attend Denton Bible Church.

Stacie Ruth Stoelting and Bright Light Ministry share how to have victory over tragedies. At fifteen, Stacie Ruth wrote *Still Holding Hands,* depicting her grandparents' romance, and victory over Alzheimer's. At twenty, she sang for President Bush. Now she speaks, acts, sings, and writes books. Visit her Web site at www.brightlightministry.com.

Aaron Swavely writes devotionals for the *Upper Room.* He works full time as a courier in Valley Forge, Pennsylvania. He and his wife, Amy, have been married for eighteen years and have three children.

Ken Wales is a graduate of USC Cinema School, where he is an adjunct professor. With credits on over fifty films including *The Tamarind Seed, Revenge of the Pink Panther, Island in the Stream*, and *Wild Rovers*, Ken was also the executive producer of the beloved CBS series *Christy*. Most recently, he produced the critically acclaimed feature film *Amazing Grace*, the compelling story of William Wilberforce. Known for his quest to further Christian values in Hollywood, Ken is also a sought-after speaker and author.

McNair Wilson has lived his life in the visual and theatre arts—and the church. As a Disney Imagineer he was on design teams for five new Disney theme parks and numerous attractions and resort experiences. He is a leading consultant in creative problem solving and brainstorming, delivering keynote addresses and workshops at professional conventions worldwide. McNair's most recent book is *Raised in Captivity: A Memoir of a Life Long Churchaholic*. Visit his Web sites at www.teawithmcnair.typepad.com and www.mcnairwilson.com.

SOURCES

Chambers, Oswald. *My Utmost for His Highest.* Grand Rapids: Discovery House Publishers, 1992. Used by permission. All rights reserved.

"A Chip Off the 'Andy' Block" excerpted and modified from Gelsinger, Pat. *Balancing Your Family, Faith, and Work.* Colorado Springs: Life Journey, David C. Cook, 2003.

Jackson, Gordon S. *Never Scratch a Tiger with a Short Stick.* Colorado Springs: NavPress, 2003. Used by permission. All rights reserved.

Kelly, Bob. *Worth Repeating: More Than 5,000 Classic and Contemporary Quotes.* Grand Rapids: Kregel Publications, 2003. Used by permission. All rights reserved.

SEND US YOUR STORIES!

SEND US YOUR SIMPLE LITTLE WORDS SHORT STORY NOW!

WE'D LOVE TO HEAR FROM YOU.

Send each submission in the body of the e-mail instead of as an attachment. Submit only one story per e-mail. Please refer to *Simple Little Words* in the subject line.

Send us 500 to 1,500 words explaining how someone's simple little words touched your life forever. Use the chapters in this book as examples. Submissions should be double-spaced, with 1-inch margins and 12-point Times New Roman font. Please don't bother with fancy formatting, photos, or graphics.

At the top of the first page of your story, include the date, your first and last name, complete mailing address, home phone, cell phone, e-mail address, and fax number if available. Also provide a title for your submission and total word count. That would really help us out. Submit your touching true story to michellescox@aol.com.

If your story is selected, you will receive a permissions form, which must be signed and returned. If your story is included in an upcoming book, you will receive one complimentary copy of the book, a mention in the contents page, plus a byline, a short biographical write-up, and the opportunity to purchase additional copies from the publisher at a discounted rate.

Thanks so much,
Michelle and John

DISCUSSION QUESTIONS

Please visit our Web site at www.simplelittlewords.com to find questions for your small-group study or your book-discussion group.

HONOR BOOKS

EXPRESSIONS OF FAITH, HOPE, AND LOVE

Pleasant words are like *a honeycomb,*
Sweetness to the soul and health to the bones.

PROVERBS 16:24

Let the words of my mouth and the meditation of my heart
Be acceptable in Your sight,
O LORD, my strength and my Redeemer.

PSALM 19:14

A soft answer turns away wrath,
But a harsh word stirs up anger.

PROVERBS 15:1

Lord, open my eyes to see the people in my life who
desperately need to hear simple little words of encouragement,
of love, or of hope. Open my heart to share generously those
special words that I might otherwise keep selfishly to myself.
Lord, open my ears to hear the words of hope and
encouragement that you are speaking to me. I humbly offer
you three simple little words: I love you. Amen.

BUT THE GREATEST OF THESE IS
LOVE!

If I speak with human eloquence and angelic ecstasy but don't love, I'm nothing but the creaking of a rusty gate. If I speak God's Word with power, revealing all his mysteries and making everything plain as day, and if I have faith that says to a mountain, "Jump," and it jumps, but I don't love, I'm nothing. If I give everything I own to the poor and even go to the stake to be burned as a martyr, but I don't love, I've gotten nowhere. So, no matter what I say, what I believe, and what I do, I'm bankrupt without love. Love never gives up. Love cares more for others than for self. Love doesn't want what it doesn't have. Love doesn't strut, doesn't have a swelled head, doesn't force itself on others, isn't always "me first," doesn't fly off the handle, doesn't keep score of the sins of others, doesn't revel when others grovel, takes pleasure in the flowering of truth, puts up with anything, trusts God always, always looks for the best, never looks back, but keeps going to the end. Love never dies. Inspired speech will be over some day; praying in tongues will end; understanding will reach its limit. We know only a portion of the truth, and what we say about God is always incomplete. But when the Complete arrives, our incompletes will be canceled. When I was an infant at my mother's breast, I gurgled and cooed like any infant. When I grew up, I left those infant ways for good. We don't yet see things clearly. We're squinting in a fog, peering through a mist. But it won't be long before the weather clears and the sun shines bright! We'll see it all then, see it all as clearly as God sees us, knowing him directly just as he knows us! *But for right now, until that completeness, we have three things to do to lead us toward that consummation: Trust steadily in God, hope unswervingly, love extravagantly. And the best of the three is love* (1 Corinthians 13:1–13 MSG).

Encourage a Weary Mom

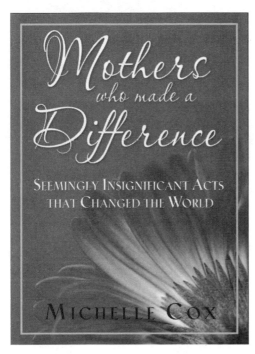

Based on examples from the Bible, *Mothers Who Made a Difference* provides touching fictional accounts that modern moms will appreciate. Each story and accompanying application demonstrates how much God values mothers. Stories provide examples of how everyday circumstances and decisions influence the lives of our children in life-changing and eternal ways.

Hardcover with Jacket
ISBN: 9781562928377
$12.99

FROM DAVID C. COOK

Celebrate What Makes a House a Home

Home—it's where we recharge our batteries, host our friends and neighbors, and nurture our familes. *Bless This Home* is a celebration of the harmony to be found when the house becomes home—with heartwarming quotations, inspiring Scriptures, soul-stirring reflections, tender prayers, and deeply moving poetry just right for reflecting on our many blessings. *Bless This Home* is perfect for housewarmings, welcoming new neighbors, or any gift-giving occasion.

Hardcover
ISBN: 9781562929527
$12.99

Return to the Simplicity and Joy of Christmas

Following the twenty-eight days of Advent, each daily entry includes a portion of the Christmas story, short devotional reflection, simple prayer, Scripture verse, and an inspirational story. Week-ending pages feature Christmas carols and hymns and ideas for Christ-centered Christmas traditions and activities any individual or family can enjoy. A wonderful gift for anyone looking to recapture the wonder and the true meaning of Christmas.

Hardcover
ISBN: 9781562928827
Retail: $12.99